How You Can Run
The Christian Race
Successfully
Looking unto Jesus

Emmanuel A. Allotey

Troubador Publishing Ltd
Unit E2 Airfield Business Park,
Harrison Road, Market Harborough,
Leicestershire. LE16 7UL
Tel: 0116 2792299
Email: books@troubador.co.uk
Web: www.troubador.co.uk

ISBN 978 1805144 113

British Library Cataloguing in Publication Data.
A catalogue record for this book is available from the British Library.

Printed and bound in Great Britain by 4edge Limited
Typeset in 11pt Adobe Caslon Pro by Troubador Publishing Ltd, Leicester, UK

Dedication

I dedicate this book to Bishop Richard Aryee and Apostle Kingsley Gyasi. Thanks for the pastoral input you have both made in my life.

Contents

CHAPTER 1

Who is a Christian According to the Bible?

King Agrippa, believest thou the prophets? I know that thou believest. Then Agrippa said unto Paul, Almost thou persuadest me TO BE A CHRISTIAN.

Acts 26:27-28

Many people profess to be Christians, but what they believe in is not based on the teachings of the Bible. Therefore, we need to learn who a true Christian is according to the Bible, which is the final authority regarding the Christian faith.

Nine Descriptions of a Christian

1. A Christian is a person who has heard the gospel of Jesus Christ or the gospel of salvation and has believed it according to John 3:16.

For God so loved the world, that he gave his only begotten Son, that whosoever believeth in him should not perish, but have everlasting life.

John 3:16

For I am not ashamed of the gospel of Christ: for it is the power of God unto salvation to everyone that believeth; to the Jew first, and also to the Greek.

Romans 1:16

Moreover, brethren, I declare unto you the gospel which I preached unto you, which also ye have received, and wherein ye stand; By which also ye are saved, if ye keep in memory what I preached unto you, unless ye have believed in vain. For I delivered unto you first of all that which I also received, how that Christ died for our sins according to the scriptures; And that he was buried, and that he rose again the third day according to the scriptures.

1 Corinthians 15:1-4

2. A Christian is a person who believes in Jesus Christ as their Saviour, that Jesus has died and saved them from their sin and hell.

And she shall bring forth a son, and thou shalt call his name Jesus: for he shall save his people from their sins.

Matthew 1:21

But now being made free from sin, and become servants to God, ye have your fruit unto holiness, and the end everlasting life. For the wages of sin is death; but the gift of God is eternal life through Jesus Christ our Lord.

Romans 6:22-23

Jesus came to save us from sin and the consequences of sin, which is death. Death is eternal separation from God in hell. Salvation is about two things: salvation from sin and the eternal punishment of sin in hell. If you believe in Jesus as your Saviour, you will not perish in hell but have everlasting life in Christ with heaven as your destination.

3. A Christian is a person who is Born Again.

Jesus answered and said unto him, Verily, verily, I say unto thee, Except a man be born again, he cannot see the kingdom of God. Nicodemus saith unto him, How can a man be born when he is old? can he enter the second time into his mother's womb, and be born? Jesus answered, Verily, verily, I say unto thee, Except a man be born of water and of the Spirit, he cannot enter into the kingdom of God.

John 3:3-6

But as many as received him, to them gave he power to become the sons of God, even to them that believe on his name: Which were born, not of blood, nor of the will of the flesh, nor of the will of man, but of God.

John 1:12-13

That if thou shalt confess with thy mouth the Lord Jesus, and shalt believe in thine heart that God hath raised him from the dead, thou shalt be saved. For with the heart man believeth unto righteousness; and with the mouth confession is made unto salvation.

Romans 10:9-10

A Christian is someone who has come to the realisation of being innately born into sin which is of the Adamic nature; and acknowledges being spiritually dead and unable to relate to God. Thus, such a person must be Born Again by accepting Jesus Christ, as their Lord and personal Saviour as stated in John 1:12-13. This is done by believing in the heart that Jesus Christ is Lord and confessing with the mouth that God raised Him from the dead.

4. A Christian is a person who follows Jesus Christ as his Lord.

Therefore let all the house of Israel know assuredly, that God hath made the same Jesus, whom ye have crucified, both Lord and Christ.

Acts 2:36

For our conversation is in heaven; from whence also we look for the Saviour, the Lord Jesus Christ.

Philippians 3:20

A Lord is someone who has authority over you. When you accept Jesus Christ as your saviour, it goes with your acceptance of Him as your Lord and therefore, what He says in His Word is what you live by daily.

5. A Christian is a person who believes and obeys the teachings of Jesus Christ.

And why call ye me, Lord, Lord, and do not the things which I say? Whosoever cometh to me, and heareth my sayings, and doeth them, I will shew you to whom he is like.

Luke 6:46-47

6. A Christian is a person who believes in the whole Bible as the Word of God.

All scripture is given by inspiration of God, and is profitable for doctrine, for reproof, for correction, for instruction in righteousness: That the man of God may be perfect, throughly furnished unto all good works.

2 Timothy 3:16-17

As a Christian, you must believe in the whole Bible to guide you and to help you do what is pleasing to God. You cannot accept Christ as your Lord, and then allow the world to teach you how to live your life. No! The Word of God must become your guide as soon as you accept Christ into your life.

5

7. A Christian is a person who is filled with the Spirit of Jesus Christ which is the Holy Spirit.

But ye are not in the flesh, but in the Spirit, if so be that the Spirit of God dwell in you. Now if any man have not the Spirit of Christ, he is none of his.

Romans 8:9

8. A Christian is a Person who is led by the Holy Spirit.

For as many as are led by the Spirit of God, they are the sons of God.

Romans 8:14

9. Christians bear the fruit of the Holy Spirit.

But the fruit of the Spirit is love, joy, peace, longsuffering, gentleness, goodness, faith, Meekness, temperance: against such there is no law.

Galatians 5:22-23

A Christian bears no other fruit but the fruit that the Spirit he is filled with produces. If you are filled with the Spirit of God then the Spirit of God will lead or influence you, and control you to do things characteristic of the Spirit. The fruit of the Spirit shows the nature of God, so if we have God then we shall also have His nature. Therefore, true Christians should always look into The Word of God to see who they are and then aim to become it. If you do not look into the Word, you will not know who God has made you to be.

CHAPTER 2

Christianity as a Race of Faith

Wherefore seeing we also are compassed about with so great a cloud of witnesses, let us lay aside every weight, and the sin which doth so easily beset us, and let us run with patience THE RACE THAT IS SET BEFORE US.

Hebrews 12:1

The Christian walk with God is a race. Christians only have a limited amount of time to live on earth and to discover and do the will of God. It can be over anytime. The Christian life is a race of faith. In 2 Timothy 4:7 (NIV), Paul described this race as a race of faith by saying, **"I have fought the good fight, I have finished the race, I have kept the faith"**. As Christians, we are to live by faith. We need to understand the nature and characteristics of this race of faith that God expects us to run.

The Nature and Characteristics of the Race of Faith

1. The Christian race of faith has a start and a finish.

> For by grace are ye SAVED THROUGH FAITH; and that not of yourselves: it is the gift of God.
>
> Ephesians 2:8

> I have fought the good fight, I have FINISHED THE RACE, I HAVE KEPT THE FAITH.
>
> 2 Timothy 4:7 (NIV)

The starting point of becoming a Christian is by exercising faith in Jesus Christ for salvation. You believe Jesus died for you and then you confess Him as your Lord and Saviour. He then imparts the Life and nature of God into your spirit man. Your spirit now becomes alive unto God, and you can henceforth commune with God, as God is a Spirit. (John

4:24). He then imparts to you the spirit of faith, for we are saved by grace through faith. At the time of salvation, God gives us a measure of faith so that we can live by faith.

> For I say, through the grace given unto me, to every man that is among you, not to think of himself more highly than he ought to think; but to think soberly, ACCORDING AS GOD HATH DEALT TO EVERY MAN THE MEASURE OF FAITH.
>
> Romans 12:3

We start this race of faith when we receive Christ as Our Lord and personal Saviour and will finish when Christ comes again or when we see Christ in heaven after death, whichever comes first. There is great joy awaiting us when we finish the race set before us. The finish line for this race is in eternity with Jesus. It is important to start a race but more importantly to finish the race and finish well. Therefore, be determined by the help of God and the Holy Spirit to finish well.

2. The Christian race of faith is personal and non-competitive.

> Hearken to me, ye that follow after righteousness, ye that seek the Lord: look unto the rock whence ye are hewn, and to the hole of the pit whence ye are digged. Look unto Abraham your father, and unto Sarah that bare you: FOR I CALLED HIM ALONE, and blessed him, and increased him.
>
> Isaiah 51:1-2

The Christian race is not a competition with others. For the Christian race, God does not call a group of people, but calls us individually and gives us specific assignments for our lives. You have a unique calling that you must discover and fulfil. We are not to compare ourselves with what others are doing or not doing. We must focus on our calling. We must compare what we are doing in the Kingdom of God with what God has called us to do for Him, and not what others are doing for Him.

> For we dare not make ourselves of the number, or compare ourselves with some that commend themselves: but they measuring themselves by themselves, and comparing themselves among themselves, are not wise.
>
> 2 Corinthians 10:12

3. The Christian race of faith has rules that govern our particular race.

> Wherefore seeing we also are compassed about with so great a cloud of witnesses, let us LAY ASIDE EVERY WEIGHT, AND THE SIN which doth so easily beset us, and let us run with patience the race that is set before us, LOOKING UNTO JESUS the author and finisher of our faith; who for the joy that was set before him endured the cross, despising the shame, and is set down at the right hand of the throne of God.
>
> Hebrews 12:1-2

Paul wrote in 2 Timothy 2:5 (NIV) saying, *"Similarly, anyone who competes as an athlete does not receive the victor's crown except by competing according to the rules"*. There are also rules governing the Christian race, which involve laying aside every weight and sin and looking unto Jesus. A weight can be a distraction or anything that slows you down in the race of faith, such as the cares of this life and selfish ambitions. Frankly speaking, self and selfish ambitions must die, or one cannot run this Christian Race successfully. Paul said, *"No man that warreth entangleth himself with the affairs of this life; that he may please him who hath chosen him to be a soldier"* (2 Timothy 2:4). Also, we must not allow sin to dominate our lives as we run the race of faith. Sin is pleasurable for a season, but it kills destinies. Sin destroyed the destiny of Samson. The Bible says clearly that sin shall not have dominion over you: for ye are not under the law, but under grace (Romans 6:14). Grace empowers you to live a pure and holy life that Christ came to purchase for us. Sin is the nature of the devil (1 John 3:8) and therefore is in rebellion against God and the Word of God. Hence, we cannot make progress in our race with a sinful lifestyle. We must choose to suffer for a while as we learn to walk in righteousness (Hebrews 11: 24-25).

Choosing rather to suffer affliction with the people of God, than to enjoy THE PLEASURES OF SIN FOR A SEASON.

Hebrews 11:25

All sin is a hindrance to Christian living, but there is a specific sin that you must watch out for. The one sin that hinders the race of faith is unbelief. It is doubting God and His word. It is this unbelief that gives birth to other sins (Hebrews 3:12).

4. The Christian race of faith requires self-control.

I therefore so run, not as uncertainly; so fight I, not as one that beateth the air: But I KEEP UNDER MY BODY, AND BRING IT INTO SUBJECTION: lest that by any means, when I have preached to others, I myself should be a castaway.

1 Corinthians 9:26-27

Christianity requires self-denial and discipline to follow Jesus. It takes daily discipline to stay in the Word of God, to learn how to know the voice of the Holy Spirit, to follow Him no matter what, amid Social Media frenzy and manipulations of the mind, for one to be a true success in the Christian Race.

5. The Christian race of faith requires endurance to finish.

Therefore, since we are surrounded by such a huge crowd of witnesses to the life of faith, let us strip off every weight that slows us down, especially the sin that so easily trips us up. And let us run with ENDURANCE the race God has set before us.

Hebrews 12:1 ((NLT)

But he that shall ENDURE unto the end, the same shall be saved.

Matthew 24:13

Remember that Jesus Christ of the seed of David was raised from the dead according to my gospel: Wherein I suffer trouble, as an evil doer, even unto bonds; but the word of God is not bound. Therefore I endure all things for the elect's sakes, that they may also obtain the salvation which is in Christ Jesus with eternal glory.

2 Timothy 2:8-10

Endurance is the power to bear pain and hardships. It is the ability or strength to continue or persevere to the end, especially despite fatigue, stress, or other adverse conditions. In this Christian race of faith, there are trials that we have to endure. Jesus endured the contradictions of sinners and the cross. Paul wrote:

Looking unto Jesus the author and finisher of our faith; who for the joy that was set before him ENDURED THE CROSS, despising the shame, and is set down at the right hand of the throne of God. For consider him that ENDURED SUCH CONTRADICTION OF SINNERS against himself, lest ye be wearied and faint in your minds.

Hebrews 12:2-3

6. The Christian race of faith has a prize at the end for those who run successfully by remaining faithful to the end.

Know ye not that they which run in a race run all, but one receiveth the prize? So run, that ye may obtain.

1 Corinthians 9:24

I press toward the mark for the prize of the high calling of God in Christ Jesus.

Philippians 3:14

There is a prize at the end of the Christian race. God will give crowns to all those who run successfully. The prize at the end of the race must motivate us just as it motivated Paul. We must aim to have crowns in heaven. Paul said:

> *I have fought a good fight, I have finished my course, I have kept the faith: Henceforth there is laid up for me A CROWN of righteousness, which the Lord, the righteous judge, shall give me at that day: and not to me only, but unto all them also that love his appearing.*
>
> *2 Timothy 4:7-8*

As a Christian, it is living the life of faith that is; living by the Word of God daily that will ensure that you finish and receive a crown. We must be faithful till the end, and God will reward us for our faithfulness. Do not just run, but run to get a prize.

CHAPTER 3

Faith Quotes

"Faith is obedience and obedience is Faith."
Dag Heward Mills

"Faith and works are bound up in the same bundle. He that obeys God trusts God; and he that trusts God obeys God. He that is without faith is without works; and he that is without works is without faith."
Charles Spurgeon

"Faith looks not at what happens to him but at Him Whom he believes."
Watchman Nee

"Faith is trust or commitment to what you think is true."
William Lane Craig

"Faith is a living and unshakable confidence, a belief in the grace of God so assured that a man would die a thousand deaths for its sake."

Martin Luther

"Faith never knows where it is being led, but it loves and knows the One who is leading."

Oswald Chambers

"If you lose faith, you lose all."

Eleanor Roosevelt

"Every day you need to get a full dose of the Word and meditate on scripture, and if you discipline yourself and remain consistent, your faith will grow and mature, and remember that God, the Word, and your faith, is a recipe for success."

Stephanie Williams

"The greatest legacy one can pass on to one's children and grandchildren is not money or other material things accumulated in one's life, but rather a legacy of character and faith."

Billy Graham

"Faith in God includes Faith in God's timing."

Neal A. Maxwell

"Christianity is not about how much faith you have. Its about Who your faith is in."

Mike Donahey

"Faith doesn't get you around problems in life and relationships, it gets you through it."

Jonathan Anthony Burkett, Friends 2 Lovers: The Unthinkable

"Fear tries to get us to give up but faith takes us all the way through to victory."

Joyce Meyer

"Faith is not something that goes against the evidence, it goes beyond it. The evidence is saying to us, 'There is another country. There is something beyond mere reason'."

Alister E. McGrath

"While you are going through your trial, you can recall your past victories and count the blessings that you do have with a sure hope of greater ones to allow if you are faithful."

Ezra Taft Benson

CHAPTER 4

What Every Christian Should Know About Jesus Christ

When Jesus came into the coasts of Caesarea Philippi, he asked his disciples, saying, Whom do men say that I the Son of man am? And they said, Some say that thou art John the Baptist: some, Elias; and others, Jeremias, or one of the prophets. He saith unto them, But whom say ye that I am? And Simon Peter answered and said, Thou art the Christ, the Son of the living God. And Jesus answered and said unto him, Blessed art thou, Simon Barjona: for flesh and blood hath not revealed it unto thee, but my Father which is in heaven.

Matthew 16:13-17

Grace and peace be multiplied unto you through the knowledge of God, and of Jesus our Lord.

2 Peter 1:2

It is important to know who Jesus Christ is. Knowing who Jesus Christ is, is foundational for our Christian faith. Also, a revelation knowledge of Jesus Christ will cause us to experience the transforming grace of God in our lives. There are many unsearchable things that we can learn about Jesus Christ.

Unto me, who am less than the least of all saints, is this grace given, that I should preach among the Gentiles THE UNSEARCHABLE RICHES OF CHRIST.

Ephesians 3:8

Twenty Things That Every Christian Should Know About Jesus Christ

1. Jesus is both the Son of God and eternal life.

And we know that THE SON OF GOD is come, and hath given us an understanding, that we may know him that is true, and we are in him that is true, EVEN IN HIS SON JESUS CHRIST. THIS IS THE TRUE GOD, AND ETERNAL LIFE.

1 John 5:20

And without controversy great is the mystery of godliness: God was manifest in the flesh, justified in the Spirit, seen of angels, preached unto the Gentiles, believed on in the world, received up into glory.

1 Timothy 3:16

The Word of God says that we can find God in Jesus Christ. This is why Jesus is the author of our Salvation. He is the One who imparts the Life of God into our spirit man at the New Birth. John 1:12 says, *"But as many as received Him, to them gave He power to become the sons of God, even to them that believe on His Name"*.

2. Jesus is the Saviour of the world.

Hereby know we that we dwell in him, and he in us, because he hath given us of his Spirit. And we have seen and do testify that the Father sent the Son to be THE SAVIOUR OF THE WORLD. Whosoever shall confess that Jesus is the Son of God, God dwelleth in him, and he in God.

1 John 4:13-15

For unto you is born this day in the city of David a Saviour, which is Christ the Lord.

Luke 2:11

3. Jesus is the author and finisher of our faith.

Looking unto Jesus THE AUTHOR AND FINISHER OF OUR FAITH; who for the joy that was set before him endured the cross, despising the shame, and is set down at the right hand of the throne of God.

Hebrews 12:2

Jesus is the originator and the one who completes our faith. Therefore, our eyes and hearts must always be fixed on Him.

4. Jesus is our justification.

> But for us also, to whom it shall be imputed, if we believe on him that raised up Jesus our Lord from the dead; Who was delivered for our offences, and was raised again for OUR JUSTIFICATION.
>
> Romans 4:24-25

Justification means to be declared free of the guilt of sin through the redemption that is in Jesus Christ. Therefore, if we are justified in Him, we have peace with God (Romans 5:1). It means that we can run well in life without feeling guilty or without living our lives as condemned sinners waiting to die and hoping to get to Heaven one day. We can live a joy-filled and faith-filled life daily, knowing that we have been justified by faith in Christ.

5. Jesus is our righteousness.

> But of him are ye in Christ Jesus, who of God is MADE UNTO US wisdom, and RIGHTEOUSNESS, and sanctification, and redemption.
>
> 1 Corinthians 1:30

> But to him that worketh not, but believeth on him that justifieth the ungodly, his faith is counted for righteousness.
>
> Romans 4:5

Jesus is our righteousness, which means He comes and lives in us and makes us righteous. We are not righteous apart from Christ. We are declared righteous by believing what Jesus did for us. Jesus does not give us righteousness; He is our righteousness. Therefore, He said to abide in Him and He in us, as we cannot bear fruit without Him or apart from Him (John 15:4).

6. Jesus is our sanctification.

But of him are ye in Christ Jesus, who of God is MADE UNTO US wisdom, and righteousness, and SANCTIFICATION, and redemption.

1 Corinthians 1:30

Unto the church of God which is at Corinth, to them that are sanctified in Christ Jesus, called to be saints, with all that in every place call upon the name of Jesus Christ our Lord, both their's and our's.

1 Corinthians 1:2

Jesus is our sanctification, which means He is the one who sanctifies or purifies us. We cannot become holy by our own efforts. We must see Jesus as our sanctifier, and then learn to live like Him.

7. Jesus is our redemption.

But of him are ye in Christ Jesus, who of God is MADE UNTO US wisdom, and righteousness, and sanctification, and REDEMPTION.

1 Corinthians 1:30

Jesus is our redemption means He bought us back by His

blood and brought us back into His image, fully restored into Him (Colossians 1:13-15).

8. Jesus is our wisdom.

> But of him are ye in Christ Jesus, who of God is MADE UNTO US WISDOM, and righteousness, and sanctification, and redemption.
>
> 1 Corinthians 1:30

9. Jesus is our peace.

> But now in Christ Jesus ye who sometimes were far off are made nigh by the blood of Christ. FOR HE IS OUR PEACE, who hath made both one, and hath broken down the middle wall of partition between us.
>
> Ephesians 2:13-14

> Therefore being justified by faith, we have peace with God through our Lord Jesus Christ.
>
> Romans 5:1

When you believe in Jesus, peace comes into your life. You are no longer guilty of sin or condemned. This is why we must live a joyful life every day by the Holy Spirit.

10. Jesus is our advocate.

> My little children, these things write I unto you, that ye sin not. And if any man sin, we have an ADVOCATE with the Father, Jesus Christ the righteous.
>
> 1 John 2:1

11. Jesus is our hope of glory.

To whom God would make known what is the riches of the glory of this mystery among the Gentiles; which is Christ in you, THE HOPE OF GLORY.

Colossians 1:27

12. Jesus is the source of our power.

But unto them which are called, both Jews and Greeks, CHRIST THE POWER of God, and the wisdom of God.

1 Corinthians 1:24

13. Jesus is the way, the truth and the life.

Jesus saith unto him, I am the way, the truth, and the life: no man cometh unto the Father, but by me.

John 14:6

When Christ, who is OUR LIFE, shall appear, then shall ye also appear with him in glory.

Colossians 3:4

Jesus is the way to be followed. He is the truth to be believed in and He is the life to come and live inside us so that we might live by His life.

14. Jesus is the resurrection and the life.

Jesus said unto her, I am the resurrection, and the life: he that believeth in me, though he were dead, yet shall he live.

John 11:25

15. Jesus is the good shepherd.

I am the good shepherd: the good shepherd giveth his life for the sheep.

John 10:11

16. Jesus is our high priest.

Seeing then that we have a great high priest, that is passed into the heavens, Jesus the Son of God, let us hold fast our profession.

Hebrews 4:14

Wherefore, holy brethren, partakers of the heavenly calling, consider the Apostle and High Priest of our profession, Christ Jesus.

Hebrews 3:1

17. Jesus is the living Word of God.

In the beginning was the Word, and the Word was with God, and the Word was God... And the Word was made flesh, and dwelt among us, (and we beheld his glory, the glory as of the only begotten of the Father,) full of grace and truth.

John 1:1,14

18. Jesus is our counsellor.

For unto us a child is born, unto us a son is given: and the government shall be upon his shoulder: and his name shall be called Wonderful, COUNSELLOR, The mighty God, The everlasting Father, The Prince of Peace.

Isaiah 9:6

19. Jesus is the baptiser with the Holy Ghost.

I indeed baptize you with water unto repentance. but he that cometh after me is mightier than I, whose shoes I am not worthy to bear: he shall BAPTIZE you with the Holy Ghost, and with fire.

Matthew 3:11

20. Jesus is our intercessor.

Who is he that condemneth? It is Christ that died, yea rather, that is risen again, who is even at the right hand of God, who also maketh intercession for us.

Romans 8:34

CHAPTER 5

What It Means to Look unto Jesus

Wherefore seeing we also are compassed about with so great a cloud of witnesses, let us lay aside every weight, and the sin which doth so easily beset us, and let us run with patience the race that is set before us, LOOKING UNTO JESUS the author and finisher of our faith; who for the joy that was set before him endured the cross, despising the shame, and is set down at the right hand of the throne of God.

Hebrews 12:1-2

As Christians, for us to run the race of faith successfully, we are to look unto Jesus, who is the greatest example of faith. Also, Jesus is the forerunner who ran the perfect race by finishing His race and lived without sinning.

Whither the forerunner is for us entered, even Jesus, made an high priest for ever after the order of Melchisedec.

Hebrews 6:20

These words spake Jesus, and lifted up his eyes to heaven, and said, Father, the hour is come; glorify thy Son, that thy Son also may glorify thee: As thou hast given him power over all flesh, that he should give eternal life to as many as thou hast given him. And this is life eternal, that they might know thee the only true God, and Jesus Christ, whom thou hast sent. I have glorified thee on the earth: I HAVE FINISHED THE WORK which thou gavest me to do.

John 17:1-4

For we have not an high priest which cannot be touched with the feeling of our infirmities; but was in all points tempted like as we are, YET WITHOUT SIN.

Hebrews 4:15

Ten Implications of Looking unto Jesus

1. To look unto Jesus implies looking to Him for salvation.

Look unto me, and be ye saved, all the ends of the earth: for I am God, and there is none else.

Isaiah 45:22

Neither is there salvation in any other: for there is none other name under heaven given among men, whereby we must be saved.

Acts 4:12

2. To look unto Jesus implies to focus on Jesus and His words.

In whom are hid all the treasures of wisdom and knowledge.

Colossians 2:3

As Christians, if we do not focus on Jesus and His words, we will miss out on the hidden treasures of wisdom and knowledge that are in Him. As you pay attention to Jesus and His words, you will learn about Him and know Him. To focus on Jesus, we must read, study, meditate and feed on the scriptures, for they testify of Him. We become like Christ as we focus on Him through His Word.

Jesus said,

Search the scriptures; for in them ye think ye have eternal life: and they are they which testify of me.

John 5:39

3. To look to Jesus implies deriving your aspirations and inspirations from Him.

Herein is our love made perfect, that we may have boldness in the day of judgment: because AS HE IS, SO ARE WE IN THIS WORLD.

1 John 4:17

We love him, because he first loved us.

1 John 4:19

For the love of Christ controls and compels us, because we have concluded this, that One died for all, therefore all died; and He died for all, so that all those who live would no longer live for themselves, but for Him who died and was raised for their sake.

2 Corinthians 5:14-15 (AMP)

As Christians, the love of Jesus should influence us to love Him and to live for Him. In life, you need a mentor, someone that you want to become like, or someone who inspires you. Jesus' goal or aspiration was to save lost humanity. Jesus' great love for souls should inspire us to sacrifice our lives for others to be saved too.

4. To look unto Jesus implies He must become your standard by following His examples.

For even hereunto were ye called: because Christ also suffered for us, leaving us an example, that ye should follow his steps.

1 Peter 2:21

In everything we do, Jesus is our best example. We are called to become disciples of Jesus. Jesus washed the disciples feet to set an example of love and service.

If I then, your Lord and Master, have washed your feet; ye also ought to wash one another's feet. For I have given you an example, that ye should do as I have done to you.

John 13:14-15

5. To look unto Jesus implies placing all your hope and confidence in Christ as your sole helper in this race of faith.

Faithful is he that calleth you, who also will do it.

1 Thessalonians 5:24

Let your conversation be without covetousness; and be content with such things as ye have: for he hath said, I will never leave thee, nor forsake thee. So that we may boldly say, THE LORD IS MY HELPER, and I will not fear what man shall do unto me.

Hebrews 13:5-6

God is faithful and He can finish what He started in you if you place your faith in Him. He has promised to be with us and never leave nor forsake us. Jesus is the author and finisher of our faith (*Hebrews 12:2*), and because Jesus ran His race and finished, He can show us the way to finish our race. Also, God never starts anything off that He is not capable of finishing. The Bible says,

Being confident of this very thing, that he which hath begun a good work in you will perform it until the day of Jesus Christ.

Philippians 1:6

Wherefore he is able also to save them to the uttermost that come unto God by him, seeing he ever liveth to make intercession for them.

Hebrews 7:25

Jesus said,

I am the vine, ye are the branches: He that abideth in me, and I in him, the same bringeth forth much fruit: FOR WITHOUT ME YE CAN DO NOTHING.

John 15:5

6. To look unto Jesus implies relying on Him to strengthen you to do all things.

I can do all things through Christ which strengtheneth me.

Philippians 4:13

7. To look unto Jesus implies trusting Him to do what you demand in His name.

And whatsoever ye shall ask in my name, that will I do, that the Father may be glorified in the Son. If ye shall ask any thing in my name, I will do it.

John 14:13-14

Then Peter said, Silver and gold have I none; but such as I have give I thee: In the name of Jesus Christ of Nazareth rise up and walk. And he took him by the right hand, and lifted him up: and immediately his feet and ankle bones received strength. And he leaping up stood, and walked, and entered with them into the temple, walking, and leaping, and praising God.

Acts 3:6-8

8. To look unto Jesus implies to accept by faith what He has done for you.

Christ hath redeemed us from the curse of the law, being made a curse for us: for it is written, Cursed is every one that hangeth on a tree: That the blessing of Abraham might come on the Gentiles through Jesus Christ; that we might receive the promise of the Spirit through faith.

Galatians 3:13-14

9. To look to Jesus implies obeying His instructions.

Now when he had left speaking, he said unto Simon, Launch out into the deep, and let down your nets for a draught. And Simon answering said unto him, Master, we have toiled all the night, and have taken nothing: nevertheless at thy word I will let down the net.

Luke 5:4-5

10. To look to Jesus implies living by the faith of Jesus.

I am crucified with Christ: nevertheless I live; yet not I, but Christ liveth in me: and the life which I now live in the flesh I LIVE BY THE FAITH OF THE SON OF GOD, who loved me, and gave himself for me.

Galatians 2:20

CHAPTER 6

Why We are to Look unto Jesus

Consider Him

LOOKING UNTO JESUS the author and finisher of our faith; who for the joy that was set before him endured the cross, despising the shame, and is set down at the right hand of the throne of God. FOR CONSIDER HIM that endured such contradiction of sinners against himself, LEST YE BE WEARIED AND FAINT IN YOUR MINDS.

Hebrews 12:2-3

W hat we look at or see affects our faith. We are to look unto Jesus in the race of faith and to consider Him so that we will not be weary and faint. The Christian race of faith is challenging. You will experience things that have the potential to make you grow weary and faint. Some trials and afflictions can make you weary and faint with time. We need to look up to Jesus to overcome discouragement, because our challenges are not greater than what He encountered. To be discouraged is to give up trying, hoping, or believing. There are many reasons why Christians become weary and faint, however, the following are just a few.

Six Reasons Why Christians Can Become Weary and Faint

1. Christians can become weary and faint due to adversity.

If thou faint in the day of adversity, thy strength is small.
Proverbs 24:10

Adversity is part of life, and everybody has a day of adversity. In this life, you will be confronted with troubles you were not expecting. There are challenges, difficulties and crises in life that have the potential to cause you to give up on your faith in God. Do not faint because of adversity. Some Christians gave up on their faith when they lost their loved ones. It is a difficult storm of life but God can strengthen you to carry on. Do not stop serving God because of adversity. The Bible says,

> Many are the afflictions of the righteous: but the Lord delivereth him out of them all.
>
> Psalm 34:19

Life is not only about achievements but also about survival. Jesus was betrayed and crucified but He endured His trials.

2. Christians can become weary and faint due to tiredness or exhaustion.

> And the apostles gathered themselves together unto Jesus, and told him all things, both what they had done, and what they had taught. And he said unto them, Come ye yourselves apart into a desert place, and rest a while: for there were many coming and going, and they had no leisure so much as to eat.
>
> Mark 6:30-31

> He giveth power to the faint; and to them that have no might he increaseth strength. Even the youths shall faint and be weary, and the young men shall utterly fall: But they that wait upon the Lord shall renew their strength; they shall mount up with wings as eagles; they shall run, and not be weary; and they shall walk, and not faint.
>
> Isaiah 40:29-31

Many Christians run around and are so busy that they do not even have time to eat or rest. Jesus believes in rest, and we must also learn to rest. Without rest, we will become exhausted and burnt out. Our busy life coupled with adversities can bring exhaustion or tiredness. Combining life with ministry work can be very demanding; therefore, we must take time off to wait upon the LORD so that our strength can be renewed.

3. Christians can become weary and faint due to lack of a prayerful lifestyle.

And he spake a parable unto them to this end, that men ought ALWAYS TO PRAY, AND NOT TO FAINT.

Luke 18:1

But thou hast not called upon me, O Jacob; but thou hast been weary of me, O Israel.

Isaiah 43:22

There are two groups of Christians; those who faint because they do not pray and those who do not pray because they have become wearied of praying. We must learn to pray a lot, especially in tongues, as praying in tongues edifies or helps to build us up. Praying in tongues charges your spirit man up like a battery, and we know that when the battery is full, you can do a lot of things with strength and ease. Therefore, pray to avoid weariness in life and ministry.

4. Christians can become weary and faint due to deferred hope.

Hope deferred maketh the heart sick: but when the desire cometh, it is a tree of life.

Proverbs 13:12

Hope is expecting something to happen at a particular time. When your heart is filled with hope, you are ready to endure anything. You need a lot of hope in the Christian race of faith. Faith is the substance of things hoped for (Hebrews 11:1). There are many things that we believe God for that will not happen immediately. We need to hold on to hope else we will give up believing. Against hope, Abraham believed in hope.

> Who against hope believed in hope, that he might become the father of many nations, according to that which was spoken, So shall thy seed be.
>
> Romans 4:18

5. Christians can become weary and faint due to unbelief.

> I had fainted, unless I had believed to see the goodness of the Lord in the land of the living.
>
> Psalm 27:13

Lack of faith in the goodness of God causes Christians to become weary and faint. This is why we must constantly feed on the goodness of God to build our trust in Him.

6. Christians can become weary and faint due to lack of Bible study and meditation on the word of God.

> Thy words were found, and I did eat them; and thy word was unto me the joy and rejoicing of mine heart: for I am called by thy name, O Lord God of hosts.
>
> Jeremiah 15:16

This book of the law shall not depart out of thy mouth; but thou shalt meditate therein day and night, that thou mayest observe to do according to all that is written therein: for then thou shalt make thy way prosperous, and then thou shalt have good success.

Joshua 1:8

The word of God is our spiritual food, and it gives us supernatural strength. *"And Jesus answered him, saying, It is written, That man shall not live by bread alone, but by every word of God" (Luke 4:4).* We must read and meditate on the word of God. Meditation gives us revelations that make us run the Christian race successfully when we apply them. Meditation also builds up our inner man. True christianity is a spiritual thing, not just a religion. As such, we must consciously and intentionally feed on the word of God for our spirit man to become strong enough to last the race.

CHAPTER 7

How to Look unto Jesus

LOOKING UNTO JESUS the author and finisher of our faith; who for the joy that was set before him endured the cross, despising the shame, and is set down at the right hand of the throne of God. FOR CONSIDER HIM that endured such contradiction of sinners against himself, lest ye be wearied and faint in your minds.

Hebrews 12:2-3

I HAVE SET THE LORD ALWAYS BEFORE ME: because he is at my right hand, I shall not be moved.

Psalm 16:8

A s Christians, we look unto Jesus by setting Him continually before us as our example, and our great encouragement in all that God has called us to do. We must consider Him and meditate upon Him.

Seven Keys on How to Look unto Jesus

1. Ask God for the spirit of revelation in the knowledge of Jesus, and search the scriptures to know Him.

That the God of our Lord Jesus Christ, the Father of glory, may give unto you the spirit of wisdom and revelation in the knowledge of him.

Ephesian 1:17

Search the scriptures; for in them ye think ye have eternal life: and they are they which testify of me.

John 5:39

From the book of Genesis to Revelation, you can see Jesus being revealed in them. It will be difficult to look to Jesus if you do not already know Him. You know Him by getting to know His nature, His divinity, and His humanity, so you can properly relate with Him.

2. Aim to become like Jesus.

For whom he did foreknow, he also did PREDESTINATE TO BE CONFORMED TO THE IMAGE OF HIS SON, that he might be the firstborn among many brethren.

Romans 8:29

It is your destiny to become more like Jesus. You must desire to become what God has purposed for your life and not just what the World has projected on you. For example, the world can project that you grow up to be a very good doctor, engineer, accountant or such like. These are all good, but God's desire is for us to become like His Son Jesus Christ. Hence, we look unto Jesus, the author and finisher of our faith.

3. Receive encouragement and guidance from the words of Jesus and His life.

These things I have spoken unto you, that in me ye might have peace. In the world ye shall have tribulation: but be of good cheer; I have overcome the world.

John 16:33

For the love of Christ constraineth us; because we thus judge, that if one died for all, then were all dead: And that he died for all, that they which live should not HENCEFORTH LIVE UNTO THEMSELVES, BUT UNTO HIM WHICH DIED FOR THEM, AND ROSE AGAIN.

2 Corinthians 5:14-15

Jesus saith unto them, My meat is to do the will of him that sent me, and to finish his work.

John 4:34

4. Do the works of Jesus.

Verily, verily, I say unto you, He that believeth on me, the works that I do shall he do also; and greater works than these shall he do; because I go unto my Father.

John 14:12

5. Seek the help and guidance of the Holy Spirit.

But when He, the Spirit of Truth, comes, He will guide you into all the truth [full and complete truth]. For He will not speak on His own initiative, but He will speak whatever He hears [from the Father—the message regarding the Son], and He will disclose to you what is to come [in the future]. He will glorify and honor Me, because He (the Holy Spirit) will take from what is Mine and will disclose it to you.

John 16:13-14 (AMP)

6. Trust Jesus with your life and future.

Do not work for food that perishes, but for food that endures [and leads] to eternal life, which the Son of Man will give you; for God the Father has authorized Him and put His seal on Him." Then they asked Him, "What are we to do, so that we may habitually be doing the works of God?" Jesus answered, "This is the work of God: that you believe [adhere to, trust in, rely on, and have faith] in the One whom He has sent."

John 6:27-29 (AMP)

7. Take the communion of the blood and body of Christ often.

I speak as to wise men; judge ye what I say. The cup of blessing which we bless, is it not the communion of the blood of Christ? The bread which we break, is it not the communion of the body of Christ?

1 Corinthians 10:15-16

Then Jesus said unto them, Verily, verily, I say unto you, Except ye eat the flesh of the Son of man, and drink his blood, ye have no life in you. Whoso eateth my flesh, and drinketh my blood, hath eternal life; and I will raise him up at the last day. For my flesh is meat indeed, and my blood is drink indeed. He that eateth my flesh, and drinketh my blood, dwelleth in me, and I in him. As the living Father hath sent me, and I live by the Father: so he that eateth me, even he shall live by me.

John 6:53-57

CHAPTER 8

How to Become More Like Jesus

For whom he did foreknow, he also did predestinate to be CONFORMED TO THE IMAGE OF HIS SON, that he might be the firstborn among many brethren.

Romans 8:29

O ur goal or purpose as Christians is to become more like Jesus Christ. For this to become possible you must:

1. Pray for Christ to be formed in you.

My little children, of whom I travail in birth again until Christ be formed in you.

Galatians 4:19

2. Grow in your knowledge of Jesus Christ.

But GROW in grace, and IN THE KNOWLEDGE OF OUR LORD AND SAVIOUR JESUS CHRIST. To him be glory both now and ever. Amen.

2 Peter 3:18

Until we all reach unity in the faith and in THE KNOWLEDGE OF THE SON OF GOD AND BECOME MATURE, attaining to the whole measure of the fullness of Christ.

Ephesians 4:13 (NIV)

We cannot grow to be like someone we do not know. We must, therefore, grow in our knowledge of Jesus Christ by studying about Him from the Scriptures and then moving on to talk to Him daily on any issue of life. For it is one thing to know about Christ and what He has done for you, and another thing to have an intimate relationship with Him. The Spirit of the Lord will change you into the image of Jesus Christ as you behold Him daily through the Scriptures and learn to talk to Him. It is a daily affair, where you grow more intimately into Him through prayer and communication. You only grow to know somebody by spending time communicating with the person.

But we all, with open face beholding as in a glass THE GLORY OF THE LORD, ARE CHANGED INTO THE SAME IMAGE from glory to glory, even as by the Spirit of the Lord.

2 Corinthians 3:18

3. Learn from Christ.

But you did not learn Christ in this way! If in fact you have [really] heard Him and have been taught by Him, just as truth is in Jesus [revealed in His life and personified in Him].

Ephesians 4:20-21 (AMP)

Come unto me, all ye that labour and are heavy laden, and I will give you rest. Take my yoke upon you, and LEARN OF ME; for I am meek and lowly in heart: and ye shall find rest unto your souls.

Matthew 11:28-29

4. Walk in Christ.

As ye have therefore received Christ Jesus the Lord, so WALK YE IN HIM: Rooted and built up in him, and stablished in the faith, as ye have been taught, abounding therein with thanksgiving.

Colossians 2:6-7

For in him we live, and move, and have our being; as certain also of your own poets have said, For we are also his offspring.

Acts 17:28

After the New Birth, that is, after you have received Jesus Christ into your heart, you must then begin to grow and learn how to walk in Him. You can walk in Christ as you are in Christ and Christ is in you. Furthermore, you are joined to Him and are one spirit with Him. *"But he that is joined unto the Lord is one spirit" (1 Corinthians 6:17).* You need to know and declare who you are in Christ. Speaking and declaring what God says about your new nature helps to solidify it into your spirit man and then it becomes your reality.

5. Have the mind of Christ.

Let this mind be in you, which was also in Christ Jesus.

Philippians 2:5

6. Have the humility of Christ.

Take my yoke upon you. Let me teach you, because I am humble and gentle at heart, and you will find rest for your souls.

Matthew 11:29 (NLT)

And being found in fashion as a man, he humbled himself, and became obedient unto death, even the death of the cross.

Philippians 2:8

7. Have the gentleness of Christ.

Now I Paul myself beseech you by the meekness and gentleness of Christ, who in presence am base among you, but being absent am bold toward you.

2 Corinthians 10:1

8. Have the patience of Christ.

I John, who also am your brother, and companion in tribulation, and in the kingdom and patience of Jesus Christ, was in the isle that is called Patmos, for the word of God, and for the testimony of Jesus Christ.

Revelation 1:9

9. Have the faithfulness of Christ.

And from Jesus Christ, who is the faithful witness, and the first begotten of the dead, and the prince of the kings of the earth. Unto him that loved us, and washed us from our sins in his own blood.

Revelation 1:5

Wherefore, holy brethren, partakers of the heavenly calling, consider the Apostle and High Priest of our profession, Christ Jesus; Who was faithful to him that appointed him, as also Moses was faithful in all his house.

Hebrews 3:1-2

10. Have the faith of Christ.

And the grace of our Lord was exceeding abundant with FAITH and love which is in Christ Jesus.

1 Timothy 1:14

11. Have the love of Christ.

For the love of Christ constraineth us; because we thus judge, that if one died for all, then were all dead.

2 Corinthians 5:14

And walk in love, as Christ also hath loved us, and hath given himself for us an offering and a sacrifice to God for a sweetsmelling savour.

Ephesians 5:2

12. Have the compassion of Christ.

And Jesus went about all the cities and villages, teaching in their synagogues, and preaching the gospel of the kingdom, and healing every sickness and every disease among the people. But when he saw the multitudes, HE WAS MOVED WITH COMPASSION on them, because they fainted, and were scattered abroad, as sheep having no shepherd.

Matthew 9:35-36

13. Be merciful like Christ.

But when Jesus heard that, he said unto them, They that be whole need not a physician, but they that are sick. But go ye and learn what that meaneth, I WILL HAVE MERCY, and not sacrifice: for I am not come to call the righteous, but sinners to repentance.

Matthew 9:12-13

14. Have the peace of Christ.

Peace I leave with you, my peace I give unto you: not as the world giveth, give I unto you. Let not your heart be troubled, neither let it be afraid.

John 14:27

15. Have the zeal of Christ.

And said unto them that sold doves, Take these things hence; make not my Father's house an house of merchandise. And his disciples remembered that it was written, The zeal of thine house hath eaten me up.

John 2:16-17

16. Have the will of Christ for oneness amongst Christians.

And now I am no more in the world, but these are in the world, and I come to thee. Holy Father, keep through thine own name those whom thou hast given me, THAT THEY MAY BE ONE, as we are.

John 17:11

17. Love righteousness and hate iniquity like Christ.

But unto the Son he saith, Thy throne, O God, is for ever and ever: a sceptre of righteousness is the sceptre of thy kingdom. THOU HAST LOVED RIGHTEOUSNESS, AND HATED INIQUITY; therefore God, even thy God, hath anointed thee with the oil of gladness above thy fellows.

Hebrews 1:8-9

18. Have the joy of Christ.

These things have I spoken unto you, that my joy might remain in you, and that your joy might be full.

John 15:11

What It Means to Become Like Jesus Christ

1. To have the nature of Christ.

But ye have not so LEARNED CHRIST; If so be that ye have heard him, and have been taught by him, as the truth is in Jesus: That ye put off concerning the former conversation the old man, which is corrupt according to the deceitful lusts; And be renewed in the spirit of your mind; And that ye PUT ON THE NEW MAN, which after God is CREATED IN RIGHTEOUSNESS AND TRUE HOLINESS.

Ephesians 4:20-24

The nature of Christ is righteousness and true holiness. We must learn to consciously put on Christ daily by declaring what God says we are in Christ.

2. To have the life of Christ.

I am crucified with Christ: nevertheless I live; yet not I, but Christ liveth in me: and the life which I now live in the flesh I live by the faith of the Son of God, who loved me, and gave himself for me.

Galatians 2:20

3. To be conformed to the image of Christ.

For whom he did foreknow, he also did predestinate to be conformed to the image of his Son, that he might be the firstborn among many brethren.

Romans 8:29

When people see you, they must see Christ. As Christians, Christ must be formed in us. Paul prayed for the Galatians that Christ would be formed in them.

My little children, of whom I travail in birth again until Christ be formed in you.

Galatians 4:19

CHAPTER 9

Becoming and Making Disciples of Jesus

Then said Jesus to those Jews which BELIEVED on him, If ye continue in my word, then are ye my DISCIPLES indeed.

John 8:31

Jesus came and told HIS DISCIPLES, "I have been given all authority in heaven and on earth. Therefore, go and MAKE DISCIPLES of all the nations, baptizing them in the name of the Father and the Son and the Holy Spirit. Teach these new disciples to obey all the commands I have given you. And be sure of this: I am with you always, even to the end of the age."

Matthew 28:18-20 (NLT)

J esus called us to be disciples. You can believe in Jesus, but you are not yet a disciple (John 8:31). There is a difference between a believer and a disciple. We must go beyond believing to become disciples. A true Christian is a disciplined follower of Christ. Hence, Christianity is about becoming a disciple of Christ. A disciple is a disciplined or committed follower of Christ. It is after becoming a disciple of Christ that you can make disciples of Christ, as you cannot give what you do not have. Unfortunately, there are not many true disciples today, as many new converts do not develop into disciples of Christ. Disciples live to learn from their master, Jesus, and to become like Him. Many Christians are not living the life of a disciple either, because they have not been properly taught the difference or they simply are not serious about their walk with The Lord.

Becoming a disciple of Christ requires a high level of commitment and devotion, which one must give themselves to without exception.

Ten Marks of a True Disciple of Jesus Christ

1. A mark of a disciple of Jesus Christ is that the person is a serious student of the Word of God.

Study to shew thyself approved unto God, a workman that needeth not to be ashamed, rightly dividing the word of truth.

2 Timothy 2:15

Search the scriptures; for in them ye think ye have eternal life: and they are they which testify of me.

John 5:39

It is written in the prophets, And they shall be all taught of God. Every man therefore that hath heard, and hath learned of the Father, cometh unto me.

John 6:45

Three days later they found Him in the [court of the] temple, sitting among the teachers, both listening to them and asking them questions. All who heard Him were amazed by His intelligence and His understanding and His answers.

Luke 2:46-47 (AMP)

Serious students of the Bible take time and effort to have a complete understanding of God's Word. Jesus studied the Word, He quoted from the old testaments. He sat among teachers to discuss the scriptures. If you do not study the Word, you will not know and follow the Words of Jesus. In the Bible, the disciples of Jesus quoted from the book of Joel on the day of Pentecost. Peter said,

But this is that which was spoken by the prophet Joel; And it shall come to pass in the last days, saith God, I will pour out of my Spirit upon all flesh: and your sons and your daughters shall prophesy, and your young men shall see visions, and your old men shall dream dreams: And on my servants and on my handmaidens I will pour out in those days of my Spirit; and they shall prophesy: And I will shew wonders in heaven above, and signs in the earth beneath; blood, and fire, and vapour of smoke: The sun shall be turned into darkness, and the moon into blood, before the great and notable day of the Lord come: And it shall come to pass, that whosoever shall call on the name of the Lord shall be saved.

Acts 2:16-21

As students or disciples of Christ, we are to know the LORD Jesus, be taught by Him and grow up into Him. Make Bible study a lifelong pursuit. Read the Bible regularly and consistently. Like a treasure hunt, believers must diligently explore the depths of God's Word.

2. A mark of a disciple of Jesus Christ is that the person has become like Christ.

The disciple is not above his master: but every one that is perfect SHALL BE AS HIS MASTER.

Luke 6:40

A student is not superior to his teacher; but everyone, after he has been completely trained, will be like his teacher.

Luke 6:40 (AMP)

The main goal of a disciple is to become like their master, so your main purpose as a disciple of Christ should be Christlikeness. When you become like Jesus, the world will know that you are a Christian or follower of Jesus. Furthermore, you can represent Him and His message to the world.

Now when they saw the boldness of Peter and John, and

perceived that they were unlearned and ignorant men, they marvelled; and they took knowledge of them, that they had been with Jesus.

Acts 4:13

3. A mark of a disciple of Jesus Christ is that the person loves God more than anything else including themselves.

If any man come to me, and hate not his father, and mother, and wife, and children, and brethren, and sisters, yea, and his own life also, he cannot be my disciple.

Luke 14:26

In the above verse, the Greek word translated as hate is the word "Miseo", which also means "to love less". What the verse means is that if you want to follow Jesus, your love for your father, mother, wife, children and yourself must be less than the love you have for Jesus. You must love God more than anything else in your life, including yourself. Jesus said, "He that loveth father or mother more than me is not worthy of me: and he that loveth son or daughter more than me is not worthy of me" (Matthew 10:37).

You must be devoted to following Jesus more than anyone else, even our closest family and friends. Jesus must become our first and highest love. Possibly the biggest obstacle to new believers going on to become disciples is their relationships. You cannot follow the LORD if your family, friends or even your personal needs and desires come first. You must be willing to deny all of these in order for you to follow on to know The Lord intimately.

4. A mark of a disciple of Jesus Christ is that the person lives a daily life of sacrifice.

And he said to them all, If any man will come after me, let him deny himself, and take up his cross daily, and follow me. For whosoever will save his life shall lose it: but whosoever will lose his life for my sake, the same shall save it.

Luke 9:23-24

A true disciple takes up their cross every day, which means we die daily to anything and everything that would distract or divert us from following the LORD wholeheartedly. A disciple lives a life of sacrifice, not pursuing their own desires but denying them to take up their cross to follow Jesus. To live for ourselves is the path to losing our lives. For even the highest earthly goals bring only fleeting satisfaction and then emptiness. We were created for God's pleasure, and therefore only a life devoted to this will ever fulfil us. To live the life of sacrifice we are called to is the path to the most fulfilling life of all.

When Jesus called His disciples, it was for total commitment. They had to be willing to leave everything to follow Him, and so are we. If He is not the LORD of all, then He is not the LORD at all. Every time you see the cross, you must remember the price that was paid for our salvation. Jesus paid the price, and you will also have to pay a price to follow Him. Paul said, *"For unto you it is given in the behalf of Christ, not only to believe on him, but also to suffer for his sake" (Philippians 1:29).*

A sacrifice is the act of losing something. When you are a living sacrifice, it means you are no longer your own. Paul said,

I beseech you therefore, brethren, by the mercies of God, that ye present your bodies a living sacrifice, holy, acceptable unto God, which is your reasonable service.

Romans 12:1

5. A mark of a disciple of Jesus Christ is that the person has surrendered everything that He owns to God.

So likewise, whosoever he be of you that forsaketh not all that he hath, he cannot be my disciple.

Luke 14:33

Neither was there any among them that lacked: for as many as were possessors of lands or houses sold them, and brought the prices of the things that were sold, And laid them down at the apostles' feet: and distribution was made unto every man according as he had need.

Acts 4:34-35

A disciple does not have an ownership mentality, but that of a steward. All that we have we receive from God, and we must be willing to give it and use it for God's work whenever He demands it. The Bible says, *"For who maketh thee to differ from another? and what hast thou that thou didst not receive? now if thou didst receive it, why dost thou glory, as if thou hadst not received it? (1 Corinthians 4:7).*

6. A mark of a disciple of Jesus Christ is that the person loves the brethren.

A NEW COMMANDMENT I give unto you, That ye LOVE ONE ANOTHER; AS I HAVE LOVED YOU,

that ye also love one another. By this shall all men know
that ye are MY DISCIPLES, if ye have love one to another.

John 13:34-35

This is my commandment, That ye love one another, as I
have loved you. Greater love hath no man than this, that a
man lay down his life for his friends.

John 15:12-13

Jesus loved the brethren and hence gave a new
commandment for all disciples to be taught and to follow
this commandment of loving the brethren. As Christians, we
are to love the brethren as Christ loved us. Christ loved us
more than He loved His own life. He laid down His life
for us, and that is how He now commands us to love one
another. You are to love all the brethren and not some.

7. A mark of a disciple of Jesus Christ is that the person forgives.

And be ye kind one to another, tenderhearted, forgiving one
another, even as God for Christ's sake hath forgiven you.

Ephesians 4:32

It is natural not to forgive as an unbeliever. A Christian
is a brand-new person or a spiritually alive person in Christ,
with the ability to forgive and walk in forgiveness. Therefore,
we must forgive others just as God has forgiven us. God
forgave us whilst we were yet sinners. Those who offend us do
not need to say sorry to us before we forgive them. We must
forgive them without conditions. As a Christian, you do not

have a right not to forgive someone. Colossians 3:12-13 says, "Put on therefore, as the elect of God, holy and beloved, bowels of mercies, kindness, humbleness of mind, meekness, longsuffering; Forbearing one another, and forgiving one another, if any man have a quarrel against any: even as Christ forgave you, so also do ye".

8. A mark of a disciple of Jesus Christ is that the person continues in the Word of God and in constant fellowship with The Person of The Holy Spirit.

Then said Jesus to those Jews which believed on him, If ye continue in my word, then are ye my disciples indeed.

John 8:31

There is therefore now no condemnation to them which are in Christ Jesus, who walk not after the flesh, but after the Spirit…That the righteousness of the law might be fulfilled in us, who walk not after the flesh, but after the Spirit. For they that are after the flesh do mind the things of the flesh; but they that are after the Spirit, the things of the Spirit.

Romans 8:1,4-5

It is one thing to become a disciple. It is another thing to continue as a disciple to the end. To continue in the Word means to continue studying and walking in obedience to the Word of God, and in constant fellowship with The Person of The Holy Spirit; one cannot make a success of this Christian walk without a constant fellowship with the Word and the Holy Spirit. A disciple should therefore grow in loving, studying, memorising and obeying the Word of God and learn how to talk to the Holy Spirit as a person; that means be Spirit-led, not just sensual or allow yourself to be led by your carnal senses. Again, grow in fellowship with the Word and the Spirit of God as a person.

9. A mark of a disciple of Jesus Christ is that the person bears much fruit.

> Herein is my Father glorified, that ye bear much fruit; so shall ye be my disciples.
>
> John 15:8

Not only do disciples bear fruit, but they bear "much fruit". Fruit, much fruit, is the natural consequence of being a disciple and continuing as a disciple. When a disciple obeys the LORD in all things, he will bear much fruit.

Fruitfulness is a very important part of Christianity. Every Christian must aim to be a fruitful Christian. You must bear fruits after your kind. Bearing fruit is to produce something that looks like you. You are a Christian and therefore, must produce other Christians as your fruits in the Lord.

a. To be fruitful you must have a vision to be a fruitful Christian.

> Where there is no vision, the people perish: but he that keepeth the law, happy is he.
>
> Proverbs 29:18

> Ye have not chosen me, but I have chosen you, and ordained you, that ye should go and bring forth fruit, and that your

fruit should remain: that whatsoever ye shall ask of the Father in my name, he may give it you.

John 15:16

Have a vision to be fruitful because you have been chosen to be fruitful.

b. To be fruitful you must have a strong conviction about the reality of hell.

There was a certain rich man, which was clothed in purple and fine linen, and fared sumptuously every day: And there was a certain beggar named Lazarus, which was laid at his gate, full of sores, And desiring to be fed with the crumbs which fell from the rich man's table: moreover the dogs came and licked his sores. And it came to pass, that the beggar died, and was carried by the angels into Abraham's bosom: the rich man also died, and was buried; And in hell he lift up his eyes, being in torments, and seeth Abraham afar off, and Lazarus in his bosom. And he cried and said, Father Abraham, have mercy on me, and send Lazarus, that he may dip the tip of his finger in water, and cool my tongue; for I am tormented in this flame. But Abraham said, Son, remember that thou in thy lifetime receivedst thy good things, and likewise Lazarus evil things: but now he is comforted, and thou art tormented. And beside all this, between us and you there is a great gulf fixed: so that they which would pass from hence to you cannot; neither can they pass to us, that would come from thence. Then he said, I pray thee therefore, father, that thou wouldest send him to my father's house: For I have five brethren; that he may testify unto them, lest they also come into this place of torment. Abraham saith unto him, They have Moses and the prophets; let them hear them. And he said, Nay, father Abraham: but if one went unto them from the dead, they will repent. And he said unto him, If they hear not Moses and the prophets, neither will they be persuaded, though one rose from the dead.

Luke 16:19-31

c. To be fruitful you must do the work of an evangelist.

But watch thou in all things, endure afflictions, do the work of an evangelist, make full proof of thy ministry.

2 Timothy 4:5

d. To be fruitful you must die to self and live a sacrificial Christian life.

Verily, verily, I say unto you, Except a corn of wheat fall into the ground and die, it abideth alone: but if it die, it bringeth forth much fruit.

John 12:24

e. To be fruitful you must be a prayerful Christian.

Who hath heard such a thing? who hath seen such things? Shall the earth be made to bring forth in one day? or shall a nation be born at once? for as soon as Zion travailed, she brought forth her children.

Isaiah 66:8

f. To be fruitful you must overcome procrastination and excuses.

Say not ye, There are yet four months, and then cometh harvest? behold, I say unto you, Lift up your eyes, and look on the fields; for they are white already to harvest.

John 4:35

10. A mark of a disciple of Jesus Christ is that the person does not commit sin.

He that committeth sin is of the devil; for the devil sinneth from the beginning. For this purpose the Son of God was manifested, that he might destroy the works of the devil. WHOSOEVER IS BORN OF GOD DOTH NOT COMMIT SIN; for his seed remaineth in him: and he cannot sin, because he is born of God.

1 John 3:8-9

Anyone who deliberately and habitually practices some kind of sin has failed the test of discipleship and must repent immediately and sincerely. They must then learn how to develop their spiritual senses to walk in the spirit, for this is the only way by which to overcome sin. Romans 6:13-14 says, *"Neither yield ye your members as instruments of unrighteousness unto sin: but yield yourselves unto God, as those that are alive from the dead, and your members as instruments of righteousness unto God. For sin shall not have dominion over you: for ye are not under the law, but under grace"*. God's Grace is there to empower you to live a sin-free holy life unto God. To be a disciple, you must therefore, forsake all sin and make an unreserved commitment to Jesus Christ (2 Timothy 2:19).

CHAPTER 10

Why You Must Be a Committed Christian

Master, which is the great commandment in the law?
Jesus said unto him, Thou shalt love the Lord thy God
with all thy heart, and with all thy soul, and with all
thy mind. This is the first and great commandment.

Matthew 22:36-38

He that hath my commandments, and keepeth them,
he it is that loveth me: and he that loveth me shall
be loved of my Father, and I will love him, and will
manifest myself to him.

John 14:21

Christianity is about having a relationship with God. Commitment is vital in every relationship. As Christians, loving God requires commitment hence, we must not compromise our commitment to God. Committing to anything in life can be challenging. However, it takes commitment to make progress or do well in every aspect of life. Commitment is the state or quality of dedication to a cause. We are to be committed or dedicated to the cause of knowing, loving, and serving God. Therefore, a lack of commitment is possibly due to a lack of interest in God and conviction.

Thirteen Reasons Why You Must Be a Committed Christian

1. You must be a committed Christian because God deserves your commitment.

We love him, because he first loved us.

1 John 4:19

For the love of Christ constraineth us; because we thus judge, that if one died for all, then were all dead: And that he died for all, that they which live should not henceforth live unto themselves, but unto him which died for them, and rose again.

2 Corinthians 5:14-15

When we think deeply about what God has done for

us; His love and salvation towards us, then sacrificing our lives for Him becomes a reasonable service. *"I beseech you therefore, brethren, by the mercies of God, that ye present your bodies a living sacrifice, holy, acceptable unto God, which is your reasonable service" (Romans 12:1).* God deserves to be loved by us as a result, loving and serving God should not become a compulsion. He deserves our commitment because He first loved us and showed us what true love is.

The one who has been forgiven many times loves much. We express our love and gratitude to God through our devotion to Him. Jesus appreciated the love showed Him by the woman with an alabaster box of ointment by saying that,

> Wherefore I say unto thee, Her sins, which are many, are forgiven; for she loved much: but to whom little is forgiven, the same loveth little.
>
> Luke 7:47

2. You must be a committed Christian because God demands your commitment.

> And God spake all these words, saying, I am the Lord thy God, which have brought thee out of the land of Egypt, out of the house of bondage. Thou shalt have no other gods before me.
>
> Exodus 20:1-3

> And when he had called the people unto him with his disciples also, he said unto them, Whosoever will come after me, let him deny himself, and take up his cross, and follow me.
>
> Mark 8:34

3. You should be a committed Christian who is not a hearer of the Word only as you will be deceiving yourself.

But be ye doers of the word, and not hearers only, deceiving your own selves.

James 1:22

And why call ye me, Lord, Lord, and do not the things which I say?

Luke 6:46

As a Christian, you must be determined to live a life controlled by the Word of God. That is by following the instructions of God through His Word and His Spirit. You cannot walk in true love towards God without doing what He says. "My little children, let us not love in word, neither in tongue; but in deed and in truth" (1 John 3:18).

4. Your commitment or lack of commitment can as a Christian become an example that others may follow.

Simon Peter saith unto them, I GO A FISHING. THEY SAY UNTO HIM, WE ALSO GO WITH THEE. They went forth, and entered into a ship immediately; and that night they caught nothing.

John 21:3

Let no one look down on [you because of] your youth, but BE AN EXAMPLE AND SET A PATTERN for the believers in speech, in conduct, in love, in faith, and in [moral] purity.

1 Timothy 4:12 (AMP)

As a Christian, know and understand that your life and commitment to God can inspire or influence others to become committed too, so be a good role model for others to follow. There is always somebody who looks up to you whether you know it or not, hence it is important for you to set good examples for others.

5. Jesus cannot effectively live His life through you when you are not a committed Christian.

I am crucified with Christ: nevertheless I live; yet not I, but CHRIST LIVETH IN ME: and the life which I now live in the flesh I live by the faith of the Son of God, who loved me, and gave himself for me.

Galatians 2:20

As Christians, we are the body of Christ, and He operates through us to touch and affect lives on earth. In the book of Acts, we find the Apostles praying for God to stretch forth His hands to heal and do mighty works, but God used their hands to bring that to pass.

And now, Lord, behold their threatenings: and grant unto thy servants, that with all boldness they may speak thy word, By STRETCHING FORTH THINE HAND TO HEAL; and that signs and wonders may be done by the name of thy holy child Jesus.

Acts 4:29-30

And by THE HANDS OF THE APOSTLES WERE MANY SIGNS AND WONDERS WROUGHT among the people; (and they were all with one accord in Solomon's porch.

Acts 5:12

6. Be a committed Christian because your labour is not in vain in the Lord.

Therefore, my beloved brethren, BE YE STEDFAST, UNMOVEABLE, always abounding in the work of the Lord, forasmuch as ye know that YOUR LABOUR IS NOT IN VAIN IN THE LORD.

1 Corinthians 15:58

And I heard a voice from heaven saying unto me, Write, Blessed are the dead which die in the Lord from henceforth: Yea, saith the Spirit, that they may rest from their labours; and THEIR WORKS DO FOLLOW THEM.

Revelation 14:13

There are many things we have achieved on earth that will be in vain when we die. It is only our works in the LORD that will follow us after death. Our wealth and possessions cannot follow us. Hence, we must use our wealth to serve God so that we can have real treasures in Heaven.

7. Be a committed Christian so that you can develop a closer relationship with God which is a good thing.

DRAW NIGH TO GOD, AND HE WILL DRAW NIGH TO YOU. Cleanse your hands, ye sinners; and purify your hearts, ye double minded.

James 4:8

But it is GOOD FOR ME TO DRAW NEAR TO GOD: I have put my trust in the Lord God, that I may declare all thy works.

Psalm 73:28

Without commitment, you cannot develop a closer relationship with God because you must seek God with all your heart to find Him and know that He is real (Jeremiah 29:13). We must seek God with all our hearts to find Him because He is a God who hides Himself (Isaiah 45:15). We must desire and develop a closer relationship with God because He created us to have fellowship with Him. Many things in life tend to hinder us from drawing nigh to God and hence we must be determined to develop a closer relationship with God. Your commitment will lead you to spend more time with God.

8. Be a committed Christian to ensure God's deliverance in the day of trouble.

BECAUSE HE HATH SET HIS LOVE UPON ME, THEREFORE WILL I DELIVER HIM: I will set him on high, because he hath known my name. He shall call upon me, and I will answer him: I will be with him in TROUBLE; I WILL DELIVER HIM, and honour him.

Psalm 91:14-15

Then the king arose very early in the morning, and went in haste unto the den of lions. And when he came to the den, he cried with a lamentable voice unto Daniel: and the king spake and said to Daniel, O Daniel, servant of the living God, IS THY GOD, WHOM THOU SERVEST CONTINUALLY, ABLE TO DELIVER THEE FROM THE LIONS? Then said Daniel unto the king, O king, live for ever. MY GOD HATH SENT HIS ANGEL, AND HATH SHUT THE LIONS' MOUTHS, that they have not hurt me: forasmuch as before him innocency was found in me; and also before thee, O king, have I done no hurt.

Daniel 6:19-22

9. Be a committed Christian because Commitment is a key to becoming a fruitful Christian.

I am the Vine; you are the branches. The one who remains in Me and I in him bears much fruit, for [otherwise] apart from Me [that is, cut off from vital union with Me] you can do nothing.

John 15:5 (AMP)

As Christians, God expects fruits from us. Jesus said, "Ye have not chosen me, but I have chosen you, and ordained you, that ye should go and bring forth fruit, and that your fruit should remain: that whatsoever ye shall ask of the Father in my name, he may give it you" (John 15:16). However, it takes commitment or years of faithfulness to God and spiritual activities for us to bear fruit. You must stay connected to Jesus, who is the vine and draw on His power to bear fruit. There are Christians who have gifts and talents but are not fruitful due to a lack of commitment. We must pay the price of commitment so that we can bear much fruit and bring glory to God, as well as prove that we are true disciples of Christ.

Jesus said,

Herein is my Father glorified, that ye bear much fruit; so shall ye be my disciples.

John 15:8

10. Be a committed Christian as commitment will help you stay in Christ and flourish.

If ye abide in me, and my words abide in you, ye shall ask what ye will, and it shall be done unto you.

John 15:7

Those that be planted in the house of the Lord shall flourish in the courts of our God.

Psalm 92:13

Anyone who is not committed to their local church will ultimately leave the church, which is the Body of Christ, and may leave Christ completely. An uncommitted Christian is a potential backslider. Commitment is a decision. Every Christian must be planted in the house of God so that they can flourish spiritually and materially. Jesus said that those who remain in Him and His words in them will have answers to their prayers. Also, Jesus said:

But seek ye first the kingdom of God, and his righteousness; and all these things shall be added unto you.

Matthew 6:33

11. Be a committed Christian because the way you are serving God will determine the way your children and grandchildren will serve God.

When I call to remembrance the unfeigned faith that is in thee, which dwelt first in thy grandmother Lois, and thy mother Eunice; and I am persuaded that in thee also.

2 Timothy 1:5

In life, children do what they see their parents do more than what their parents tell them to do. When our children see us serving God not out of convenience but commitment, they are likely to grow up doing the same and their future relationship with God can be guaranteed. The Bible says, "Train up a child in the way he should go: and when he is old, he will not depart from it" (Proverbs 22:6). You train a child not only by giving instructions but, more importantly, by example. We must care about the spiritual well-being and future of our children and generations after us, not just the here and now. What is the point of giving birth to a child for the child to become a devil worshipper or end up in hell? We must be diligent to consciously raise godly seeds unto God (Malachi 2:14-15). I believe strongly that this is one of the main reasons why God instructs us not to marry unbelievers. So we can train our children in the ways of God.

12. Be a committed Christian because God expects you to be busy serving Him with your talents till Jesus returns or till death.

He said: "A man of noble birth went to a distant country to have himself appointed king and then to return. So he called ten of his servants and gave them ten minas. 'PUT THIS MONEY TO WORK,' HE SAID, 'UNTIL I COME BACK'.

Luke 19:12-13 (NIV)

Fear none of those things which thou shalt suffer: behold, the devil shall cast some of you into prison, that ye may be tried; and ye shall have tribulation ten days: BE THOU FAITHFUL UNTO DEATH, and I will give thee a crown of life.

Revelation 2:10

13. Be a committed Christian because you are a part of the body of Christ and have something to supply to the growth of the body of Christ.

For as we have many members in one body, and all members have not the same office: So we, being many, are one body in Christ, and every one members one of another. Having then gifts differing according to the grace that is given to us, whether prophecy, let us prophesy according to the proportion of faith; Or ministry, let us wait on our ministering: or he that teacheth, on teaching; Or he that exhorteth, on exhortation: he that giveth, let him do it with simplicity; he that ruleth, with diligence; he that sheweth mercy, with cheerfulness.

Romans 12:4-8

From whom the whole body fitly joined together and compacted by that which EVERY JOINT SUPPLIETH, according to the effectual working in the measure of every part, maketh increase of the body unto the edifying of itself in love.

Ephesians 4:16

CHAPTER 11

Those Who Draw Back from Faith

NOW THE JUST SHALL LIVE BY FAITH: BUT IF ANY MAN DRAW BACK, my soul shall have no pleasure in him. But we are not of them who draw back unto perdition; but of them that believe to the saving of the soul.

Hebrews 10:38-39

The Christian race challenges and trials have the potential to cause some Christians to draw back from living a life of faith in God. However, drawing back from the life of faith displeases God, hence we must endeavour to persevere and finish the race of faith that we have been called to run. There are many reasons why we should not draw back from a life of faith in God, and the following are just a few.

Seven Reasons Why You Should Not Draw Back from Living by Faith

1. Those who draw back from living by faith become murmurers.

How long shall I bear with this evil congregation, which murmur against me? I have heard the murmurings of the children of Israel, which they murmur against me. Say unto them, As truly as I live, saith the Lord, as ye have spoken in mine ears, so will I do to you: Your carcases shall fall in this wilderness; and all that were numbered of you, according to your whole number, from twenty years old and upward which have murmured against me. Doubtless ye shall not come into the land, concerning which I sware to make you dwell therein, save Caleb the son of Jephunneh, and Joshua the son of Nun.

Numbers 14:27-30

God hears our murmurings and sees it as evil because it is a sign that we are doubting His faithfulness and ability to do what He has promised to do for us. Most of the Israelites, expect Caleb and Joshua, doubted God's promise to give them the land of Canaan because giants were occupying the land. Those who doubted and murmured against God were not allowed to enter the land. We must not draw back from living by faith to become murmurers, as this is evil in the sight of God, and will cause us to miss the blessings of God for our lives. The antidote for murmuring is asking. Ask, and it shall be given you (Matthew 7:7).When you doubt God, you automatically believe the lie of the devil more than you believe God and His Word. And so, God cannot stand doubters. Doubt is a very serious sin before God, and we must deal with it by feeding on the Word of God. That means any area of your life that you find you are doubting God in, locate His Word concerning that area, and feed on it as long as it takes for your faith to grow in that area. For as soon as your faith grows in that area, doubt will automatically disappear. For example, if you doubt God in the area of healing, then locate 1 Peter 2:24 and feed on it until your faith becomes strong, then healing will manifest automatically.

> Neither murmur ye, as some of them also murmured, and were destroyed of the destroyer.
>
> 1 Corinthians 10:10

2. Those who draw back from living by faith become complainers.

And when the people complained, it displeased the Lord:

and the Lord heard it; and his anger was kindled; and the fire of the Lord burnt among them, and consumed them that were in the uttermost parts of the camp.

Numbers 11:1

Like murmuring, God hears our complaints, and it displeases Him. As Christians, we must refrain from doing things that God is not pleased with.

3. Those who draw back from living by faith become lovers of this world.

For Demas hath forsaken me, having LOVED THIS PRESENT WORLD, and is departed unto Thessalonica; Crescens to Galatia, Titus unto Dalmatia.

2 Timothy 4:10

Love not the world, neither the things that are in the world. If any man love the world, the love of the Father is not in him.

1 John 2:15

Friendship with the world is enmity with God (James 4:4). We are in the world, but not of the world (John 17:14). Christianity is about being separated unto Jesus. Without separation, you cannot follow Jesus. We cannot obey the great commandment, which is loving God with all our heart, soul and mind, if we become lovers of the world. Loving the world will displace our love for God as we turn to seek after things that we love. Furthermore, what you love, you trust; hence, if you love the world, you will trust the world's way of living and doing things as opposed to how God and His Kingdom is run.

4. Those who draw back from living by faith will lose their lives.

For whosoever will save his life shall lose it; but whosoever shall lose his life for my sake and the gospel's, the same shall save it. For what shall it profit a man, if he shall gain the whole world, and lose his own soul? Or what shall a man give in exchange for his soul?

Mark 8:35-37

5. Those who draw back from living by faith are usually influenced by demons.

Now the feast of unleavened bread drew nigh, which is called the Passover. And the chief priests and scribes sought how they might kill him; for they feared the people. THEN ENTERED SATAN INTO JUDAS surnamed Iscariot, being of the number of the twelve. And he went his way, and communed with the chief priests and captains, how he might betray him unto them.

Luke 22:1-4

6. Those who draw back from living by faith become lukewarm Christians.

I know thy works, that thou art neither cold nor hot: I would thou wert cold or hot. So then because thou art lukewarm, and neither cold nor hot, I will spue thee out of my mouth.

Revelation 3:15-16

Lukewarmness is a very dangerous lifestyle to have as a Christian, where you are neither cold nor hot. But you must choose to be a hot Christian who is always on fire for God. So, pray for fresh fire every day.

7. Those who draw back from living by faith lose their position or office to others.

"Go out and stand before me on the mountain," the Lord told him. And as Elijah stood there, the Lord passed by, and a mighty windstorm hit the mountain. It was such a terrible blast that the rocks were torn loose, but the Lord was not in the wind. After the wind there was an earthquake, but the Lord was not in the earthquake. And after the earthquake there was a fire, but the Lord was not in the fire. And after the fire there was the sound of a gentle whisper. When Elijah heard it, he wrapped his face in his cloak and went out and stood at the entrance of the cave. And a voice said, "WHAT ARE YOU DOING HERE, ELIJAH?" He replied again, "I have zealously served the Lord God Almighty. But the people of Israel have broken their covenant with you, torn down your altars, and killed every one of your prophets. I AM THE ONLY ONE LEFT, AND NOW THEY ARE TRYING TO KILL ME, TOO." Then the Lord told him, "Go back the same way you came, and travel to the wilderness of Damascus. When you arrive there, anoint Hazael to be king of Aram. Then anoint Jehu grandson of Nimshi to be king of Israel, and anoint Elisha son of Shaphat from the town of Abel-meholah to REPLACE YOU AS MY PROPHET.

1 Kings 19:11-16 (NLT)

Refuse to draw from living by faith by becoming a firebrand. Let no man take your place in God's Kingdom. Choose to sense God with zeal until the end.

CHAPTER 12

Overcoming Trials
of Faith

Blessed be the God and Father of our Lord Jesus Christ, which according to his abundant mercy hath begotten us again unto a lively hope by the resurrection of Jesus Christ from the dead, To an inheritance incorruptible, and undefiled, and that fadeth not away, reserved in heaven for you, Who are kept by the power of God through faith unto salvation ready to be revealed in the last time. Wherein ye greatly rejoice, though now for a season, if need be, ye are in heaviness through manifold temptations: That THE TRIAL OF YOUR FAITH, being much more precious than of gold that perisheth, though it be tried with fire, might be found unto praise and honour and glory at the appearing of Jesus Christ.

1 Peter 1:3-7

To him that overcometh will I grant to sit with me in my throne, even as I also overcame, and am set down with my Father in his throne.

Revelation 3:21

A s Christians, our faith in God and His Word shall be tested. Tests and trials are to be expected because those who live godly shall suffer persecution (*2 Timothy 3:12*) and God allows our faith in Him to be tested. God may allow trials of our faith so that He can expose what is in our hearts for us to know ourselves. We cannot be certain of our responses to the trials of our faith till we experience them. We always have a choice to make as to how we respond to the challenges of life and faith in God. It is also through trials and tests that we can prove the word of God. You become strong in faith only when you are tried.

> Remember how the Lord your God led you all the way in the wilderness these forty years, to humble and TEST YOU IN ORDER TO KNOW WHAT WAS IN YOUR HEART, whether or not you would keep his commands.
>
> Deuteronomy 8:2 (NIV)

Trials can be opportunities for us to trust God and for God to reveal His power and nature in us, so we can grow in Him. Trials test our faith and ability to trust in God. Without trials, a born-again child of God will never truly grow up in Christ. It is the trials of our faith that produce patience, love, long-suffering and such like in the believer. James 1:3 says, *"Knowing this, that the trying of your faith worketh patience"*. So, believers must learn to embrace trials, as these only help us to use our faith in the Word. Faith is like a muscle, and unless it is exercised daily, it will lie dormant and be very flabby. Faith is not just head knowledge or information about a particular Word of God but it is how to use that Word in times of trials. So, trials are very good for the believer. Learn to factor trials into your walk with God, do not see them as stumbling blocks but as stepping stones. When in trial focus on the word of God, not the problem, and you will come out quicker and stronger.

Thirteen Ways to Overcome the Trials of Your Faith

1. Overcome trials of faith by being joyful in hope.

BE JOYFUL IN HOPE, patient in affliction, faithful in prayer.

Romans 12:12 (NIV)

CONSIDER IT PURE JOY, my brothers and sisters, whenever you face trials of many kinds.

James 1:2 (NIV)

Being intentionally joyful during trials of faith is important because the joy of the LORD is your strength (*Nehemiah 8:10*). Without strength, you cannot resist the enemy and overcome troubles. Failing on a day of adversity is because of small strength. Proverbs 24:10 says, *"If thou faint in the day of adversity, thy strength is small"*. You must be hopeful during trials because Christ in you the hope of glory (Colossians 1:27). Whatever you are experiencing in life is temporal, and therefore you can hope that things will change by the grace of God as you stand by the word of God.

For our light affliction, which is but FOR A MOMENT, worketh for us a far more exceeding and eternal weight of glory.

2 Corinthians 4:17

2. Overcome trials of faith by being patient in affliction.

Be joyful in hope, PATIENT IN AFFLICTION, faithful in prayer.

Romans 12:12 (NIV)

Knowing this, that the trying of your faith worketh patience. But let patience have her perfect work, that ye may be perfect and entire, wanting nothing.

James 1:3-4

Patience is a fruit of the Spirit that must be developed in our lives as Christians. We develop patience during challenging times when we learn to endure and persevere as Christians. We must keep believing God's word in such times, and when we are patient in affliction, God will deliver us from all our afflictions and our needs shall be met. The Bible says. *"Many are the afflictions of the righteous: but the Lord delivereth him out of them all" (Psalm 34:19).* Impatience will cause you to give up on God and your dreams before they come to pass.

Cast not away therefore your confidence, which hath great recompence of reward. For YE HAVE NEED OF PATIENCE, that, after ye have done the will of God, ye might receive the promise.

Hebrews 10:35-36

3. Overcome trials of faith by being faithful in prayer.

Be joyful in hope, patient in affliction, FAITHFUL IN PRAYER.

Romans 12:12 (NIV)

And he spake a parable unto them to this end, that men ought always to pray, and not to faint.

Luke 18:1

Is any among you afflicted? let him pray. Is any merry? let him sing psalms.

James 5:13

Being faithful in prayer is a key to overcoming trials of faith. Prayer is talking to God and listening to what He has to say to us. Sometimes trials of faith persist because we are not listening to God when we pray, we pray religiously about our challenges without waiting to hear what God has to say. Matthew 7:7-8 says, "Ask, and it shall be given you; seek, and ye shall find; knock, and it shall be opened unto you: For every one that asketh receiveth; and he that seeketh findeth; and to him that knocketh it shall be opened". We must develop the art of praying and waiting to hear what God has to tell us so that we can know what to do to experience deliverance from our trials. God answers prayers, so we should expect a word from God when we pray.

I will stand upon my watch, and set me upon the tower, and will watch to see WHAT HE WILL SAY UNTO ME, and what I shall answer when I am reproved. AND THE LORD ANSWERED ME, and said, Write the vision, and make it plain upon tables, that he may run that readeth it. For the vision is yet for an appointed time, but at the end it shall speak, and not lie: though it tarry, wait for it; because it will surely come, it will not tarry.

Habakkuk 2:1-3

Daniel was faithful in prayer when his faith in God was tested. He steadfastly prayed three times a day (*Daniel 6:10*). Daniel's steadfast faith in God, during his trials, was rewarded when God preserved his life in the lion's den and God was glorified. God rewards those who diligently seek Him.

4. Overcome trials of faith by being thankful.

In every thing give thanks: for this is the will of God in Christ Jesus concerning you.

1 Thessalonians 5:18

Save us, O Lord our God, and gather us from among the heathen, TO GIVE THANKS UNTO THY HOLY NAME, AND TO TRIUMPH IN THY PRAISE.

Psalm 106:47

It is very easy to give thanks to God when things are going on well for us, but very difficult to give thanks in hard times, even though God's Word says that in everything, give thanks. As unpleasant as trials are, there are still many reasons for giving thanks.

a. **In everything give thanks because there is always something to be thankful to God for even in a bad situation, at least it could have been worse.**

We are troubled on every side, YET NOT DISTRESSED; we are perplexed, but NOT IN DESPAIR; Persecuted, but NOT FORSAKEN; cast down, but NOT DESTROYED.

2 Corinthians 4:8-9

b. **In everything give thanks because all things will work together for your good.**

And we know that all things work together for good to them that love God, to them who are the called according to his purpose.

Romans 8:28

c. **In everything give thanks because that is God's Will and plan of deliverance.**

And brought them to the magistrates, saying, These men, being Jews, do exceedingly trouble our city, And teach customs, which are not lawful for us to receive, neither to observe, being Romans. And the multitude rose up together against them: and the magistrates rent off their clothes, and commanded to beat them. And when they had laid many stripes upon them, they cast them into prison, charging the jailor to keep them safely: Who, having received such a charge, thrust them into the inner prison, and made their feet fast in the stocks. And at midnight Paul and Silas prayed, and SANG PRAISES UNTO GOD: and the prisoners heard them. And suddenly

THERE WAS A GREAT EARTHQUAKE, SO THAT THE FOUNDATIONS OF THE PRISON WERE SHAKEN: AND IMMEDIATELY ALL THE DOORS WERE OPENED, AND EVERY ONE'S BANDS WERE LOOSED.

Acts 16:20-26

d. In everything give thanks because we are expected to walk by faith and not by sight.

For we walk by faith, not by sight.

2 Corinthians 5:7

And being not weak in faith, HE CONSIDERED NOT HIS OWN BODY NOW DEAD, when he was about an hundred years old, neither yet the deadness of Sarah's womb: He staggered not at the promise of God through unbelief; but was strong in faith, GIVING GLORY TO GOD; And being fully persuaded that, what he had promised, he was able also to perform.

Romans 4:19-21

Giving thanks in difficult times helps you to trust God, even when you do not understand why something difficult is happening.

e. In everything give thanks because your worries will be replaced with the peace of God.

Don't worry about anything; instead, pray about everything. Tell God what you need, and thank him for all he has done. Then you will experience God's peace, which exceeds anything we can understand. His peace will guard your hearts and minds as you live in Christ Jesus.

Philippians 4:6-7 (NLT)

5. Overcome trials of faith by feeding and exercising your faith regularly.

So then faith cometh by hearing, and hearing by the word of God.

Romans 10:17

For whatsoever is born of God overcometh the world: and this is THE VICTORY THAT OVERCOMETH THE WORLD, EVEN OUR FAITH.

1 John 5:4

During adversity, decide to fight the good fight of faith. There is no victory without a battle. Faith is acting on what you believe. You must speak words of faith and victory during challenging times. Paul said, *"We having the same spirit of faith, according as it is written, I believed, and therefore have I spoken; we also believe, and therefore speak" (2 Corinthians 4:13).* You must hold fast to your confession of faith, knowing that God is faithful to fulfil His promises. Faithfully declare the promises of God over the area of your life where you are facing trials.

Let us hold fast the profession of our faith without wavering; (for he is faithful that promised).

Hebrews 10:23

Through faith also Sara herself received strength to conceive seed, and was delivered of a child when she was past age, because SHE JUDGED HIM FAITHFUL WHO HAD PROMISED.

Hebrews 11:11

6. Overcome the trials of faith by building your life on the Word of God.

Therefore whosoever heareth these sayings of mine, and doeth them, I will liken him unto a wise man, which built his house upon a rock: And the rain descended, and the floods came, and the winds blew, and beat upon that house; and it fell not: for it was founded upon a rock. And every one that heareth these sayings of mine, and doeth them not, shall be likened unto a foolish man, which built his house upon the sand: And the rain descended, and the floods came, and the winds blew, and beat upon that house; and it fell: and great was the fall of it.

Matthew 7:24-27

Jesus is likening us to a house that is built on a rock or solid foundation of the Word of God. We therefore build our lives through hearing and doing the Word of God. When you build your life on the Word and you experience the storms of life represented in the above verse as rain, floods and winds against your life, you will stand or overcome them.

7. Overcome the trials of faith with a vow to God.

Then said Elkanah her husband to her, Hannah, why weepest thou? and why eatest thou not? and why is thy heart grieved? am not I better to thee than ten sons? So Hannah rose up after they had eaten in Shiloh, and after they had drunk. Now Eli the priest sat upon a seat by a post of the temple of the Lord. And she was in bitterness of soul, and prayed unto the Lord, and wept sore. AND SHE VOWED A VOW, AND SAID, O LORD OF HOSTS, IF THOU WILT INDEED LOOK ON THE AFFLICTION OF THINE HANDMAID, AND REMEMBER ME, AND NOT FORGET THINE HANDMAID, BUT WILT GIVE UNTO THINE HANDMAID A MAN CHILD, THEN I WILL GIVE HIM UNTO THE LORD ALL THE DAYS OF HIS LIFE, AND THERE SHALL NO RAZOR COME UPON HIS HEAD.

1 Samuel 1:8-11

8. Overcome the trials of faith by asking God for wisdom to overcome those trials.

Consider it pure joy, my brothers and sisters, whenever you face trials of many kinds, because you know that the testing of your faith produces perseverance. Let perseverance finish its work so that you may be mature and complete, not lacking anything. IF ANY OF YOU LACKS WISDOM, YOU SHOULD ASK GOD, who gives generously to all without finding fault, and it will be given to you.

James 1:2-5 (NIV)

If the iron be blunt, and he do not whet the edge, then must he put to more strength: but WISDOM IS PROFITABLE TO DIRECT.

Ecclesiastes 10:10

When you ask God for wisdom, you are asking for direction to overcome the trials.

9. **Overcome the trials of faith by understanding the root cause of your trials so that you can respond appropriately.**

And as Jesus passed by, he saw a man which was blind from his birth. And his disciples asked him, saying, Master, WHO DID SIN, this man, or his parents, that he was born blind? Jesus answered, Neither hath this man sinned, nor his parents: but that the works of God should be made manifest in him.

John 9:1-3

The trials we experience in life may be because of our sinful choices or an attack from Satan. It could also be God allowing us to go through them for Him to reveal His power in us when we trust Him. Knowing the root cause or the source of our adversities in life is important so that we can act appropriately. When Satan attacked Job, Job thought God caused all the things that were destroyed in his life.

And there came a messenger unto Job, and said, The oxen were plowing, and the asses feeding beside them: And the Sabeans fell upon them, and took them away; yea, they have slain the servants with the edge of the sword; and I only am escaped alone to tell thee. While he was yet speaking, there came also another, and said, The fire of God is fallen from heaven, and hath burned up the sheep, and the servants, and consumed them; and I only am escaped alone to tell thee. While he was yet speaking, there came also another, and said, The Chaldeans made out three bands, and fell upon the camels, and have carried them away, yea, and slain the servants with the edge of the sword; and I only am escaped alone to tell thee. While he was yet speaking, there came also another, and said, Thy sons and thy daughters were eating and drinking wine in their eldest brother's house: And, behold, there came a great wind from the wilderness, and smote the four corners of the house, and it fell upon the young men, and they are dead; and I only am escaped alone to tell thee. Then Job arose, and rent his mantle, and shaved his head, and fell down upon the ground, and worshipped, And said, Naked came I out of my mother's womb, and naked shall I return thither: THE LORD GAVE, AND THE LORD HATH TAKEN AWAY; BLESSED BE THE NAME OF THE LORD.

Job 1:14-21

10. Overcome the trials of faith by the blood of Jesus and the word of your testimony.

And they overcame him by the blood of the Lamb, and by the word of their testimony; and they loved not their lives unto the death.

Revelation 12:11

There is power in the blood of Jesus and in our testimony. As Christians, we are to testify about what God has done for us through Jesus Christ. The Bible says, "Let the redeemed of the Lord say so, whom he hath redeemed from the hand of the enemy" (Psalm 107:2). We are victorious Christians because Jesus has won the victory over our invisible enemies, but we must enforce His victory in the earth. Declaring what the Word of God says about us and our circumstances brings victory into our lives because God will always perform His Word.

God is not a man, that he should lie; neither the son of man, that he should repent: hath he said, and shall he not do it? or hath he spoken, and shall he not make it good?

Numbers 23:19

Now thanks be unto God, which always causeth us to triumph in Christ, and maketh manifest the savour of his knowledge by us in every place.

2 Corinthians 2:14

11. Overcome the trials of faith by Judging God to be faithful, and ask Him to give you strength to overcome.

Through faith also SARA HERSELF RECEIVED STRENGTH to conceive seed, and was delivered of a child when she was past age, BECAUSE SHE JUDGED HIM FAITHFUL WHO HAD PROMISED.

Hebrews 11:11

There hath no temptation taken you but such as is common to man: BUT GOD IS FAITHFUL, who will not suffer you to be tempted above that ye are able; but will with the temptation also make a way to escape, that ye may be able to bear it.

1 Corinthians 10:13

Notwithstanding the Lord stood with me, and strengthened me; that by me the preaching might be fully known, and that all the Gentiles might hear: and I was delivered out of the mouth of the lion.

2 Timothy 4:17

Judging God to be faithful during trials will produce hope and strength to continue fighting the good fight of faith until victory comes. Have faith in the faithfulness of God, for He will never fail you as you put your trust in Him.

12. Overcome the trials of faith by believing in who God says you are in Christ and acting accordingly.

Ye are of God, little children, and have overcome them: because GREATER IS HE THAT IS IN YOU, THAN HE THAT IS IN THE WORLD.

1 John 4:4

Who shall separate us from the love of Christ? shall tribulation, or distress, or persecution, or famine, or nakedness, or peril, or sword? As it is written, For thy sake we are killed all the day long; we are accounted as sheep for the slaughter. Nay, in all these things WE ARE MORE THAN CONQUERORS THROUGH HIM THAT LOVED US.

Romans 8:35-37

As a child of God, exercise your faith and declare that you have overcome because the Greater One is in you. Declare that you are more than a conqueror through Jesus Christ.

13. Overcome the trials of faith by relying on the Greater One in you; the Holy Spirit for guidance to know what to say and do in the face of oppositions to your destiny.

Ye are of God, little children, and have overcome them: because greater is he that is in you, than he that is in the world.

1 John 4:4

But when they shall lead you, and deliver you up, take no thought beforehand what ye shall speak, neither do ye premeditate: but whatsoever shall be given you in that hour, that speak ye: for it is not ye that speak, but the Holy Ghost.

Mark 13:11

CHAPTER 13

Keep the Faith

I have fought a good fight, I have finished my course,
I HAVE KEPT THE FAITH.

2 Timothy 4:7

As a Christian, you must purpose to keep the faith, which means you must continue to believe and trust God and His Word, even when it is difficult to do so. It is a challenge to believe till the end, because as you go through life, your faith will be tested. One thing we must remember is that in this fallen world, everybody will go through, and are already going through difficulties, trials and afflictions of some sort. However, the beauty of true Christianity is that The Bible assures us that whatever is born of God overcomes the World (1 John 5:4). Hence, we must keep the faith regardless of the trials and afflictions that we face in life. Paul kept the faith despite perils and persecutions. Our faith in God and His word is something worth keeping because it is precious.

> Simon Peter, a servant and an apostle of Jesus Christ, to them that have obtained like PRECIOUS FAITH with us through the righteousness of God and our Saviour Jesus Christ.
>
> 2 Peter 1:1

How to Keep the Faith

1. You must be a fighter to keep the faith.

> I HAVE FOUGHT a good fight, I have finished my course, I have kept the faith.
>
> 2 Timothy 4:7

As a Christian, you must fight and purpose in your heart to keep the faith. The devil is after your faith, and hence there is a need to fight for what you believe in (Luke 22:31-32). You must fight by holding firmly on to the truth of the Word for a given situation until it manifests.

2. You must be a finisher to keep the faith.

I have fought a good fight, I HAVE FINISHED my course, I have kept the faith.

2 Timothy 4:7

As a Christian, you must aim to finish whatever good work that God has called you to do in His kingdom. Paul said, *"For we are his workmanship, created in Christ Jesus unto good works, which God hath before ordained that we should walk in them" (Ephesians 2:10)*. Many Christians do not know what they are supposed to be doing here on earth as believers. Many think that Christianity is only to be practiced in church on Sundays and, as a result, never grow beyond their Sunday attendance and maybe reading their Bibles and praying to only ask God for things that they need. This mode of thinking has affected a lot of older Christians and Christians who were somehow wealthy prior to knowing or accepting Christ. They usually do not know what to pray for when 'their needs seem to have been met'. You need to know your purpose and destiny in Christ. You are to seek God for Him to reveal any specific purpose He has for your life besides His general purposes for all Christians as revealed in the Bible. Therefore, you need to pray that the eyes of your understanding be enlighten so you will know what the hope of His calling is (Ephesians 1:17-18). There is a general will of God for all Christians revealed in the Bible, and there is a specific will of God for you to pursue at specific times of your life on earth. You must have the determination to finish any specific assignment given to you by God so that trials do not move you from it.

> Save that the Holy Ghost witnesseth in every city, saying that bonds and afflictions abide me. But NONE OF THESE THINGS MOVE ME, neither count I my life dear unto myself, SO THAT I MIGHT FINISH MY COURSE with joy, and the ministry, which I have received of the Lord Jesus, to testify the gospel of the grace of God. And now, behold, I know that ye all, among whom I have gone preaching the kingdom of God, shall see my face no more.
>
> Acts 20:23-25

3. You need to have faith and a strong conviction in order to keep the faith.

> I HAD FAINTED, UNLESS I HAD BELIEVED to see the goodness of the Lord in the land of the living.
>
> Psalm 27:13

To keep the faith, you need to have faith in the Word of God. God has a path or specific plan for your life. It requires trust and obedience to find the path that God has for you, and it requires faith and obedience to stay on that path. Sometimes, we question our path because it is filled with hardships and difficulties. However, just because things are not going the way you expect does not mean it is not God's will. As mentioned earlier, your faith is supposed to be exercised in the Word, so whenever you face opposition in your faith walk, use the Word, speak the Word into that situation until you see the desired change. You will see your faith growing stronger and stronger after every opportunity that you get to use the Word. You may not always understand the path that God has chosen for you but you can know that God is good. He loves you and He will never leave you nor forsake you. The Bible says in Hebrews 13:5-6, *"Let your conversation be without covetousness; and be content with such things as ye have: for he hath said, I will never leave thee, nor forsake thee. So that we may boldly say, The Lord is my helper, and I will not fear what man shall do unto me"*. The Apostle Paul also said,

> And we know that all things work together for good to them that love God, to them who are the called according to his purpose.
>
> Romans 8:28

4. To keep the faith, you must see your trials of faith as light afflictions compared to the eternal glory awaiting you.

> We are troubled on every side, yet not distressed; we are perplexed, but not in despair; Persecuted, but not forsaken; cast down, but not destroyed... For our light affliction, which is but for a moment, worketh for us a far more exceeding and eternal weight of glory; While we look not

at the things which are seen, but at the things which are not seen: for the things which are seen are temporal; but the things which are not seen are eternal.

2 Corinthians 4:8-9,17-18

5. To keep the faith, you must esteem the reward for your sufferings for the sake of Christ and your revelation knowledge of Christ as greater riches than earthly and temporal things.

By faith Moses, when he was come to years, refused to be called the son of Pharaoh's daughter; Choosing rather to suffer affliction with the people of God, than to enjoy the pleasures of sin for a season; Esteeming the reproach of Christ greater riches than the treasures in Egypt: FOR HE HAD RESPECT UNTO THE RECOMPENCE OF THE REWARD.

Hebrews 11:24-26

Yea doubtless, and I count all things but loss for the excellency of the knowledge of Christ Jesus my Lord: for whom I have suffered the loss of all things, and do count them but dung, that I may win Christ.

hilippians 3:8

6. You must be faithful unto death to keep the faith.

Fear none of those things which thou shalt suffer: behold, the devil shall cast some of you into prison, that ye may be tried; and ye shall have tribulation ten days: be thou faithful unto death, and I will give thee a crown of life.

Revelation 2:10

Being faithful unto death means serving God till you die, including situations where your faithfulness may cause your death. We are not to retire from serving God, and we are not to deny the faith in the face of death. Shadrach, Meshach and Abednego exhibited faithfulness unto death to keep their faith in God (Daniel 3:15-18).

7. You must recollect past encounters to keep the faith.

And David said to Saul, Let no man's heart fail because of him; thy servant will go and fight with this Philistine. And Saul said to David, Thou art not able to go against this Philistine to fight with him: for thou art but a youth, and he a man of war from his youth. And David said unto Saul, Thy servant kept his father's sheep, and there came a lion, and a bear, and took a lamb out of the flock: And I went out after him, and smote him, and delivered it out of his mouth: and when he arose against me, I caught him by his beard, and smote him, and slew him. Thy servant slew both the lion and the bear: and this uncircumcised Philistine shall be as one of them, seeing he hath defied the armies of the living God. David said moreover, The Lord that delivered me out of the paw of the lion, and out of the paw of the bear, he will deliver me out of the hand of this Philistine. And Saul said unto David, Go, and the Lord be with thee.

1 Samuel 17:32-37

CHAPTER 14

Add To Your Faith

And beside this, giving all diligence, ADD TO YOUR FAITH virtue; and to virtue knowledge; And to knowledge temperance; and to temperance patience; and to patience godliness; And to godliness brotherly kindness; and to brotherly kindness charity. For if these things be in you, and abound, THEY MAKE YOU THAT YE SHALL NEITHER BE BARREN NOR UNFRUITFUL IN THE KNOWLEDGE OF OUR LORD JESUS CHRIST. But he that lacketh these things is blind, and cannot see afar off, and hath forgotten that he was purged from his old sins. Wherefore the rather, brethren, give diligence to MAKE YOUR CALLING AND ELECTION SURE: FOR IF YE DO THESE THINGS, YE SHALL NEVER FALL: For so an entrance shall be ministered unto you abundantly into the everlasting kingdom of our Lord and Saviour Jesus Christ.

2 Peter 1:5-11

For us to run a successful Christian race, we must add to our faith virtue, knowledge, temperance, patience, godliness, brotherly kindness and charity. These spiritual qualities will make us better Christians. Faith is the foundation upon which all qualities are to be built.

1. Add to Your Faith Virtue

Virtue means moral goodness or purity. This is important in running a successful Christian race.

> Nevertheless the foundation of God standeth sure, having this seal, The Lord knoweth them that are his. And, let every one that nameth the name of Christ depart from iniquity. But in a great house there are not only vessels of gold and of silver, but also of wood and of earth; and some to honour, and some to dishonour. If a man therefore purge himself from these, he shall be a vessel unto honour, sanctified, and meet for the master's use, and prepared unto every good work. Flee also youthful lusts: but follow righteousness, faith, charity, peace, with them that call on the Lord out of a pure heart.
>
> 2 Timothy 2:19-22

2. Add to Your Faith Knowledge

Knowledge is important in running a successful Christian race. The will of God is revealed where the word of God is known; therefore, The Word of God brings knowledge that gives direction to our faith.

My people are destroyed for lack of knowledge: because thou hast rejected knowledge, I will also reject thee, that thou shalt be no priest to me: seeing thou hast forgotten the law of thy God, I will also forget thy children.

Hosea 4:6

Jesus answered and said unto them, Ye do err, not knowing the scriptures, nor the power of God.

Matthew 22:29

The Word of God must be carefully sought out regarding any situation or issues of life in the Kingdom. Then, armed with that knowledge, one can successfully wage a good warfare in prayer against any opposition that may arise.

3. Add to Your Faith Temperance

Temperance means self-control. A Christian must learn to control himself. This is important in running a successful Christian race. You must learn to self-regulate or calm yourself down so you can always think and act in line with the word of God, even under extreme pressure.

But the fruit of the Spirit is love, joy, peace, longsuffering, gentleness, goodness, faith, Meekness, TEMPERANCE: against such there is no law.

Galatians 5:22-23

I discipline my body like an athlete, training it to do what it should. Otherwise, I fear that after preaching to others I myself might be disqualified.

1 Corinthians 9:27 (NLT)

110

4. Add to Your Faith Patience

Patience means steadfastness or perseverance. Patience is important in running a successful Christian race.

> For ye have need of patience, that, after ye have done the will of God, ye might receive the promise.
>
> Hebrews 10:36

> Wherefore seeing we also are compassed about with so great a cloud of witnesses, let us lay aside every weight, and the sin which doth so easily beset us, and let us run with patience the race that is set before us.
>
> Hebrews 12:1

5. Add to Your Faith Godliness

Godliness means to reverence God, to have a God-fearing behaviour, to have a godly character, but more importantly, to have the nature of God actively in you and your life. Godliness is important in running a successful Christian race. Simply put, be conscious of God inside you; it will make your Christianity real to you every day.

> For bodily exercise profiteth little: but godliness is profitable unto all things, having promise of the life that now is, and of that which is to come.
>
> 1 Timothy 4:8

6. Add to Your Faith Brotherly Kindness

Brotherly Kindness means brotherly love. Brotherly kindness is important in running a successful Christian race.

Be kindly affectioned one to another with brotherly love; in honour preferring one another.

Romans 12:10

If a man say, I love God, and hateth his brother, he is a liar: for he that loveth not his brother whom he hath seen, how can he love God whom he hath not seen?

1 John 4:20

But whoso hath this world's good, and seeth his brother have need, and shutteth up his bowels of compassion from him, how dwelleth the love of God in him?

1 John 3:17

7. Add to Your Faith Charity

Charity is the God kind of love, which is the unconditional love that is born of God and emanates from God. Charity is important in running a successful Christian race. A very beloved general and father of the Faith once gave a testimony of how he pastored a church where most of the church leaders were so antagonistic towards him and each other. He said how he wanted to skin them alive and hated them and their bad behaviours. But every time he had felt like fighting them physically or speaking angrily to them; he fed on 1 Corinthians 13 and Galatians 5, until he began to emanate and radiate the Love of God and soon after, they had a revival in the church.

Though I speak with the tongues of men and of angels, and have not charity, I am become as sounding brass, or a

112

tinkling cymbal. And though I have the gift of prophecy, and understand all mysteries, and all knowledge; and though I have all faith, so that I could remove mountains, and have not charity, I am nothing. And though I bestow all my goods to feed the poor, and though I give my body to be burned, and have not charity, it profiteth me nothing.

1 Corinthians 13:1-3

Faith, hope, charity, these three; but the greatest of these is charity.

1 Corinthians 13:13

CHAPTER 15

How to Live a Christian Life

Then departed Barnabas to Tarsus, for to seek Saul: And when he had found him, he brought him unto Antioch. And it came to pass, that a whole year they assembled themselves with the church, and taught much people. AND THE DISCIPLES WERE CALLED CHRISTIANS first in Antioch.

Acts 11:25-26

Furthermore then we beseech you, brethren, and exhort you by the Lord Jesus, that as ye have received of us HOW YE OUGHT TO WALK and to please God, so ye would abound more and more.

1 Thessalonians 4:1

C hristianity is a lifestyle governed by the principles of the Word of God. We need to learn how to live as Christians. It is important to know how God wants us to live as Christians. When you accept Jesus as your Saviour and Lord, you become a Christian. But after that, you must learn to live as a Christian, as being born again is just how we enter the Kingdom of God, not an end in itself.

Twenty Principles for Christian Living

1. Christians should have a daily prayer time with God.

> My voice shalt thou hear in the morning, O Lord; in the morning will I direct my prayer unto thee, and will look up.
> Psalm 5:3

> And in the morning, rising up a great while before day, he went out, and departed into a solitary place, and there prayed.
> Mark 1:35

As a Christian, you must learn to start and end every day in prayer to God. Your daily prayer time must involve:

a. Thanksgiving prayer.

> Enter into his gates with thanksgiving, and into his courts with praise: be thankful unto him, and bless his name. For the Lord is good; his mercy is everlasting; and his truth endureth to all generations.
> Psalm 100:4-5

> In every thing give thanks: for this is the will of God in Christ Jesus concerning you.
>
> 1 Thessalonians 5:18

Thank God for a new day, for your life, for your health, for His Life in you; that is your Salvation, thank Him for your family, for your work and for the opportunities you want Him to give you, to mention but a few. Thank God for the miracles of the day, thank Him for blessed opportunities to share your faith and win a lost soul to Christ, and thank God for everything. That is how to enter God's presence as you begin the day. God wants us to thank Him from the beginning of every day. That is how you start the day as a Christian.

b. Confession prayer.

> If we say that we have no sin, we deceive ourselves, and the truth is not in us. If we confess our sins, he is faithful and just to forgive us our sins, and to cleanse us from all unrighteousness. If we say that we have not sinned, we make him a liar, and his word is not in us.
>
> 1 John 1:8-10

Confession prayer is when you confess your sins to God and thank Him for forgiveness.

c. Communing with the Holy Spirit.

> The grace of the Lord Jesus Christ, and the love of God, and THE COMMUNION OF THE HOLY GHOST, be with you all. Amen.
>
> 2 Corinthians 13:14

As Christians, we must develop a very strong relationship with The Person of The Holy Spirit, by communing with Him daily. We need the Holy Spirit daily in our lives because a Christian should live by the power of the Holy Spirit. Without the Holy Spirit, you do not have any power to live a victorious life against your enemies. You need the power of the Holy Spirit every day. So, every morning, ask God to anoint you with the Holy Spirit and with power, so you can overcome the challenges of the day. It is the Holy Spirit Who will direct you as to which Word to use in each situation of life because He will bring all things to your remembrance when you learn to acknowledge Him daily. So, go on and talk to Him, like you will talk to a real person when they are in the room with you because He is that Real Person and He is with you as you read. I will encourage you to put the book down a second or two and just whisper to Him, Precious Holy Spirit, thank You that You are here with me right now. Thank You for the grace to know You personally and to talk to You daily. Thank You for the grace to walk in Your Power this day, in Jesus' Mighty Name.

How God anointed Jesus of Nazareth with the Holy Ghost and with power: who went about doing good, and healing all that were oppressed of the devil; for God was with him.

Acts 10:38

Jesus Christ went about each day doing good because of the anointing of the Holy Spirit. So, a Christian must go through the day doing good, and if you are anointed with the Holy Spirit, you will set people oppressed by the devil free by preaching to them, delivering them or leading them to Christ.

d. Request prayer.

Be careful for nothing; but in every thing by prayer and supplication with thanksgiving let your requests be made known unto God. And the peace of God, which passeth all understanding, shall keep your hearts and minds through Christ Jesus.

Philippians 4:6-7

Request prayer involves petitions and supplications. This is when you ask God to help you and do things for you. Ask for help in every area that matters to you.

Ask, and it shall be given you; seek, and ye shall find; knock, and it shall be opened unto you: For every one that asketh receiveth; and he that seeketh findeth; and to him that knocketh it shall be opened.

Matthew 7:7-8

e. Intercession prayer.

I exhort therefore, that, first of all, supplications, prayers, intercessions, and giving of thanks, be made for all men; For kings, and for all that are in authority; that we may lead a quiet and peaceable life in all godliness and honesty. For this is good and acceptable in the sight of God our Saviour.

1 Timothy 2:1-3

Intercession prayer involves interceding for others, which means praying for others. Pray for people of authority in your life.

2. Christians should read the Bible every day.

And Jesus answered him, saying, It is written, That man
shall not live by bread alone, but by every word of God.

Luke 4:4

You need the Word of God every day. God expects us to
live by His Word. You must read and study the Word of God.
Your daily Bible reading time with God should involve:

a. Reading a portion of scripture from the Bible.

Till I come, give attendance to READING, to exhortation,
to doctrine.

1 Timothy 4:13

b. Meditate on the scripture that you have read.

This book of the law shall not depart out of thy mouth; but
thou shalt meditate therein day and night, that thou mayest
observe to do according to all that is written therein: for
then thou shalt make thy way prosperous, and then thou
shalt have good success.

Joshua 1:8

You meditate by thinking about what you have read and
asking questions. Ask questions about what you have read
using interrogative words such as Why? Who? How? What?
When? Which? Whose? Whom?

For any verse that you read, some of these interrogative
words will apply. As you ask the appropriate questions and
try to find answers and search for answers with the help of
the Holy Spirit, that is how to meditate on the scripture.

c. Memorize at least a verse of scripture.

Let the word of Christ dwell in you richly in all wisdom; teaching and admonishing one another in psalms and hymns and spiritual songs, singing with grace in your hearts to the Lord.

Colossians 3:16

As you memorize scriptures, the word of God will dwell in you richly.

d. Make notes.

Moreover the Lord said unto me, Take thee a great roll, and write in it with a man's pen concerning Mahershalalhashbaz.

Isaiah 8:1

Thus speaketh the Lord God of Israel, saying, Write thee all the words that I have spoken unto thee in a book.

Jeremiah 30:2

As you meditate on the scripture that you have read, you may have some understanding or revelation that you need to note down or write down for that day. You can have records of what you have learnt, and it helps you to know the Word of God and solidifies your faith as anything you write down is likely to stick than just ordinary reading.

3. Christians are to fear God and keep His commandments.

Let us hear the conclusion of the whole matter: Fear God,

and keep his commandments: for this is the whole duty of man.

Ecclesiastes 12:13

Reverential fear of God is an attitude of respect for God's presence and the word of God. This motivates us to obey God and to shun wrong doings. "By mercy and truth iniquity is purged: and by the fear of the Lord men depart from evil" (Proverbs 16:6).

A Christian must obey the commandments of God, which have been summarised into two; love God and love your neighbour as yourself.

Master, which is the great commandment in the law? Jesus said unto him, Thou shalt love the Lord thy God with all thy heart, and with all thy soul, and with all thy mind. This is the first and great commandment. And the second is like unto it, Thou shalt love thy neighbour as thyself. On these two commandments hang all the law and the prophets.

Matthew 22:36-40

4. Christians are to serve God and serve others.

How much more shall the blood of Christ, who through the eternal Spirit offered himself without spot to God, purge your conscience from dead works to serve the living God?

Hebrews 9:14

For, brethren, ye have been called unto liberty; only use not liberty for an occasion to the flesh, but by love serve one another.

Galatians 5:13

5. Christians are to Live daily by faith.

Now the just shall live by faith: but if any man draw back, my soul shall have no pleasure in him.

Hebrews 10:38

We having the same spirit of faith, according as it is written, I believed, and therefore have I spoken; we also believe, and therefore speak.

2 Corinthians 4:13

Faith believes and speaks the word of God. You must learn to daily speak or declare the word of God over your life and circumstances.

6. Christians are to do what is right, love mercy and walk humbly with God.

No, O people, the Lord has told you what is good, and this is what he requires of you: to do what is right, to love mercy, and to walk humbly with your God.

Micah 6:8 (NLT)

7. Christians should represent Christ in whatever they do or say, depending on God and being thankful.

Whatever you do [no matter what it is] in word or deed, do everything in the name of the Lord Jesus [and in dependence on Him], giving thanks to God the Father through Him.

Colossians 3:17 (AMP)

8. Christians must put their best effort into every work that they do in life as something being done for God.

Whatever you do [whatever your task may be], work from the soul [that is, put in your very best effort], as [something done] for the Lord and not for men, knowing [with all certainty] that it is from the Lord [not from men] that you will receive the inheritance which is your [greatest] reward. It is the Lord Christ whom you [actually] serve.

Colossians 3:23-24 (AMP)

Servants, be obedient to them that are your masters according to the flesh, with fear and trembling, in singleness of your heart, as unto Christ; Not with eyeservice, as menpleasers; but as the servants of Christ, doing the will of God from the heart; With good will doing service, as to the Lord, and not to men: Knowing that whatsoever good thing any man doeth, the same shall he receive of the Lord, whether he be bond or free.

Ephesians 6:5-8

9. Christians are to look to God as the source of their provision.

After this manner therefore pray ye: Our Father which art in heaven, Hallowed be thy name. Thy kingdom come, Thy will be done in earth, as it is in heaven. GIVE US THIS DAY OUR DAILY BREAD.

Matthew 6:9-11

But my God shall supply all your need according to his riches in glory by Christ Jesus.

Philippians 4:19

10. Christians are to look to God for protection from evil.

And lead us not into temptation, but DELIVER US FROM EVIL: For thine is the kingdom, and the power, and the glory, for ever. Amen.

Matthew 6:13

11. Christians are to forgive those who offend them.

And be ye kind one to another, tenderhearted, forgiving one another, even as God for Christ's sake hath forgiven you.

Ephesians 4:32

And when ye stand praying, forgive, if ye have ought against any: that your Father also which is in heaven may forgive you your trespasses.

Mark 11:25

12. Christians are to seek God's direction in everything they do.

Trust in the Lord with all thine heart; and lean not unto thine own understanding. In all thy ways acknowledge him, and he shall direct thy paths.

Proverbs 3:5-6

13. Christians are to go to church and not forsake the assembly of the saints.

Let us hold fast the profession of our faith without wavering; (for he is faithful that promised;) And let us consider one another to provoke unto love and to good works: NOT FORSAKING THE ASSEMBLING OF OURSELVES TOGETHER, as the manner of some is; but exhorting one another: and so much the more, as ye see the day approaching.

Hebrews 10:23-25

And he came to Nazareth, where he had been brought up: and, as his custom was, he went into the synagogue on the sabbath day, and stood up for to read.

Luke 4:16

Jesus had a custom or habit of going to the synagogue on the sabbath day. As Christians, we must also have this good habit of attending church. Fellowshipping with other Christians is not optional, it is essential and hence the instruction is not to forsake it.

14. Christians are to honour God with their first fruits or tithe.

Honour the Lord with thy substance, and with the firstfruits of all thine increase: So shall thy barns be filled with plenty, and thy presses shall burst out with new wine.

Proverbs 3:9-10

The first fruits or tithe which is the tenth of your income, are needed to do the work of God. There is a blessing in honouring God with the first fruits of your increase or your tithe.

Bring ye all the tithes into the storehouse, that there may be meat in mine house, and prove me now herewith, saith the Lord of hosts, if I will not open you the windows of heaven, and pour you out a blessing, that there shall not be room enough to receive it.

Malachi 3:10

15. Christians are to remember the poor.

And when James, Cephas, and John, who seemed to be pillars, perceived the grace that was given unto me, they gave to me and Barnabas the right hands of fellowship; that we should go unto the heathen, and they unto the circumcision. Only they would that we should REMEMBER THE POOR; the same which I also was forward to do.

Galatians 2:9-10

Let him that stole steal no more: but rather let him labour, working with his hands the thing which is good, that he may have to give to him that needeth.

Ephesians 4:28

For I was an hungred, and ye gave me meat: I was thirsty, and ye gave me drink: I was a stranger, and ye took me in: Naked, and ye clothed me: I was sick, and ye visited me: I was in prison, and ye came unto me. Then shall the righteous answer him, saying, Lord, when saw we thee an hungred, and fed thee? or thirsty, and gave thee drink? When saw we thee a stranger, and took thee in? or naked, and clothed thee? Or when saw we thee sick, or in prison, and came unto thee? And the King shall answer and say unto them, Verily I say unto you, Inasmuch as ye have done it unto one of the least of these my brethren, ye have done it unto me.

Matthew 25:35-40

16. Christians must seek to do things that please God.

Furthermore then we beseech you, brethren, and exhort you by the Lord Jesus, that as ye have received of us HOW YE OUGHT TO WALK AND TO PLEASE GOD, so ye would abound more and more.

1 Thessalonians 4:1

And he that sent me is with me: the Father hath not left me alone; for I do always those things that please him.

John 8:29

17. Christians must set their affection on things above.

If ye then be risen with Christ, seek those things which are above, where Christ sitteth on the right hand of God. Set your affection on things above, not on things on the earth.

Colossians 3:1-2

18. Christians must offer their bodies as a living sacrifice to God daily.

I beseech you therefore, brethren, by the mercies of God, that YE PRESENT YOUR BODIES A LIVING SACRIFICE, HOLY, acceptable unto God, which is your reasonable service.

Romans 12:1

Forasmuch then as Christ hath suffered for us in the flesh, arm yourselves likewise with the same mind: for he that hath suffered in the flesh hath ceased from sin; That he no longer should live the rest of his time in the flesh to the lusts of men, but to the will of God. For the time past of our life may suffice us to have wrought the will of the Gentiles, when we walked in lasciviousness, lusts, excess of wine, revellings, banquetings, and abominable idolatries: Wherein they think it strange that ye run not with them to the same excess of riot, speaking evil of you: Who shall give account to him that is ready to judge the quick and the dead.

1 Peter 4:1-5

For ye know what commandments we gave you by the Lord Jesus. For this is the will of God, even your sanctification, that ye should abstain from fornication: That every one of you should know how to possess his vessel in sanctification and honour; Not in the lust of concupiscence, even as the Gentiles which know not God: That no man go beyond and defraud his brother in any matter: because that the Lord is the avenger of all such, as we also have forewarned you

128

and testified. For God hath not called us unto uncleanness, but unto holiness.

1 Thessalonians 4:2-7

As a Christian, you must sacrifice your fleshly desires to serve God. You must discipline your body. The difficult part of the Christian life is fighting the sins of the flesh, but we need to crucify the flesh to walk in the spirit. We must exercise self-control and keep our bodies under control. Galatians 5:24 says that "And they that are Christ's have crucified the flesh with the affections and lusts".

19. Christians must live for Jesus Christ.

For the love of Christ constraineth us; because we thus judge, that if one died for all, then were all dead: And that he died for all, that they which live should not henceforth live unto themselves, but unto him which died for them, and rose again.

2 Corinthians 5:14-15

20. Christians are to be witnesses for Christ and to defend our faith.

Withal praying also for us, that God would open unto us a door of utterance, to speak the mystery of Christ, for which I am also in bonds: That I may make it manifest, as I ought to speak. Walk in wisdom toward them that are without, redeeming the time. Let your speech be always with grace, seasoned with salt, that ye may know how ye ought to answer every man.

Colossians 4:3-6

But ye shall receive power, after that the Holy Ghost is come upon you: and ye shall be witnesses unto me both in Jerusalem, and in all Judaea, and in Samaria, and unto the uttermost part of the earth.

Acts 1:8

But in your hearts set Christ apart [as holy—acknowledging Him, giving Him first place in your lives] as Lord. Always be ready to give a [logical] defense to anyone who asks you to account for the hope and confident assurance [elicited by faith] that is within you, yet [do it] with gentleness and respect.

1 Peter 3:15 (AMP)

Christians are to be witnesses for Christ and to defend our faith. Apart from preaching the gospel of salvation to others, you can also witness by the way you live.

For we ourselves also were sometimes foolish, disobedient, deceived, serving divers lusts and pleasures, living in malice and envy, hateful, and hating one another. But after that the kindness and love of God our Saviour toward man appeared, Not by works of righteousness which we have done, but according to his mercy he saved us, by the washing of regeneration, and renewing of the Holy Ghost; Which he shed on us abundantly through Jesus Christ our Saviour; That being justified by his grace, we should be made heirs according to the hope of eternal life. This is a faithful saying, and these things I will that thou affirm constantly, that they which have believed in God might be careful to maintain good works. These things are good and profitable unto men.

Titus 3:3-8

About the Author

Emmanuel A. Allotey is an author and serves as a Lay Pastor of the United Denominations Originating from the Lighthouse Group of Churches (UD-OLGC) with Bishop Dag Heward-Mills as the founder. He has been a pastor for over twenty-five years. Pastor Emmanuel is a minister with a passion to help Believers in Christ develop a closer walk with Jesus Christ and to fulfil their purpose through the teaching of the Word of God.

Other Books by Emmanuel A. Allotey

**101 PRAYER POINTS FOR
CHURCH GROWTH**
This book teaches how to pray for church growth.

**HOW TO GROW IN CHRIST AND MEASURE
YOUR SPIRITUAL GROWTH**
This book is a practical guide to spiritual growth.

For additional information on Emmanuel A. Allotey's books:

E-Mail: adoteyemmanuel13@gmail.com